THE BIBLE

WHAT EVERYONE NEEDS TO KNOW®

THE BIBLE

WHAT EVERYONE NEEDS TO KNOW®

MICHAEL COOGAN

OXFORD
UNIVERSITY PRESS

OXFORD
UNIVERSITY PRESS

Oxford University Press is a department of the University of Oxford. It furthers
the University's objective of excellence in research, scholarship, and education
by publishing worldwide. Oxford is a registered trade mark of Oxford University
Press in the UK and certain other countries.

"What Everyone Needs to Know" is a registered trademark of
Oxford University Press.

Published in the United States of America by Oxford University Press
198 Madison Avenue, New York, NY 10016, United States of America.

Library of Congress Cataloging-in-Publication Data
Names: Coogan, Michael David, author.
Title: The Bible : what everyone needs to know® / Michael Coogan.
Description: New York, NY, United States of America :
Oxford University Press, 2021. | Includes bibliographical references and index.
Identifiers: LCCN 2020012864 (print) | LCCN 2020012865 (ebook) |
ISBN 9780199383047 (hardback) | ISBN 9780199383030 (paperback) |
ISBN 9780199383061 (epub)
Subjects: LCSH: Bible—Introductions.
Classification: LCC BS475.3 .C664 2020 (print) |
LCC BS475.3 (ebook) | DDC 220.6/1—dc23
LC record available at https://lccn.loc.gov/2020012864
LC ebook record available at https://lccn.loc.gov/2020012865

1 3 5 7 9 8 6 4 2

Paperback printed by LSC Communications, United States of America
Hardback printed by Bridgeport National Bindery, Inc., United States of America

For Pam, as always

CONTENTS

7 The Uses of the Bible   105

8 Biblical Concepts   121

9 Biblical Values   140

ABBREVIATIONS

BCE	Before the Common Era (the equivalent of BC)
CE	Common Era (the equivalent of AD)
CEB	Common English Bible
ch(s).	chapter(s)
EBR	*Encyclopedia of the Bible and Its Reception*
GNB	Good News Bible
KJV	King James Version (Authorized Version)
LXX	The Septuagint
MT	The Masoretic Text
NAB	New American Bible
NABRE	New American Bible, Revised Edition
NIV	New International Version
NJPS	New Jewish Publication Society Translation
NRSV	New Revised Standard Version
par.	parallel passages in the Synoptic Gospels
RSV	Revised Standard Version

A NOTE ON TRANSLITERATIONS

I have used a simplified transliteration system for Hebrew, Aramaic, and Greek that will be transparent to those familiar with the languages.

1

BIBLE AND BIBLES

What is the Bible?

The Bible is the sacred scripture of Judaism and Christianity. In its pages we encounter some of the most memorable characters in world literature: Adam and Eve, Cain and Abel, Abraham and Sarah, Jacob, Moses, Samson and Delilah, David and Bathsheba, Job, Jesus, and Paul; some of the best-known religious texts: the Ten Commandments, the Shema, Psalm 23, and the Sermon on the Mount; and some of the most important concepts in theology: covenant, chosenness, sin, atonement, and salvation. Over the ages, the Bible has also had an enormous influence on politics, on literature and the arts, and even on medicine and science.

The word "Bible" basically means "book."[1] Although usually formatted as a single book, the Bible is actually a collection of shorter books written over the course of more than a thousand years, an anthology of texts that Jews and Christians have considered especially authoritative, even inspired— "holy writ." Put simply, for Jews the Bible is a collection of some twenty-four books that by the second century CE had a special status.[2] For Christians, the Bible includes these books, and some other Jewish religious writings, which together were eventually called "the Old Testament"; to them were added another twenty-seven early Christian texts, known as "the New Testament." Behind these simple definitions, however, lie many complexities, both because of the Bible's long history of formation and because of the different faith communities that consider it canonical.

What is a canon and why is it important?

The technical term for authoritative scripture is "canon," a word that comes from the Greek word for the cane plant, whose reeds were used as measuring sticks. A canon is thus originally a ruler and thus in effect a rule.

In the study of literature, a canon is a group of texts that have a special status, that are "classics," as it were. In the study of religion, a canon is those sacred texts that have special authority for a community. A canon may be a group of texts whose components are not necessarily fixed, as in Hinduism and Buddhism, or, more narrowly, only those texts that religious authorities have recognized as authoritative sacred scripture, in other words as canonical.

But the Bible is not just one canon, but several, that to some extent overlap. The processes that led to the formation of the several biblical canons were complex and gradual, and are not fully documented. Although the basic shape of the Jewish canon was set by the second century CE, there continued to be debates around the edges about whether some books should be dropped or others added.

The same is true for the New Testament. The canonical status of a few of its books was debated, and other books that some groups considered canonical were eventually not included in it. By the late fourth century, a canon of forty-six books in the Old Testament and twenty-seven in the New Testament was the norm in western Christianity, while several eastern churches added one or more books to each.

The term "Bible," then, means different things to different religious communities. All of this is very complicated, but it is necessary to explain, because, among other reasons, it shows that the Bible is a human creation: the books that comprise it, and the order in which they occur, were not sent down from heaven.

What is the Bible in Judaism?

In Jewish tradition, the Bible has twenty-four separate books, divided into three major parts.[3] The first part, known as the *Torah* ("the teaching" or "the law"), consists of the five books of Genesis, Exodus, Leviticus, Numbers, and Deuteronomy. The second part, known as the Prophets (Hebrew *Neviim*), is further divided into the Former Prophets—Joshua, Judges, Samuel, and Kings, so called because they come first—and the Latter Prophets: the "Major Prophets" Isaiah, Jeremiah, and Ezekiel, and the Book of the Twelve "Minor Prophets," Hosea through Malachi. The third part, known as the Writings (Hebrew *Ketuvim*), contains books in many genres: Psalms, Job, Proverbs, Ruth, Song of Songs, Lamentations, Ecclesiastes, Esther, Daniel, Ezra-Nehemiah, and Chronicles. The earliest reference to these three divisions dates to the second century BCE, in the Prologue to a work called "The Wisdom of Jesus, Son of Sirach," which mentions "the Law, and the Prophets, and the other books of our ancestors."[4] In Hebrew, an acronym formed from the first letter of the names of the three parts is Tanakh (or Tanak), a frequent term for the Bible in Judaism. (See Table 1.1.)

Of these three parts, the Torah was the first to be considered authoritative scripture. By the fifth century BCE, if not before, that teaching or law was in written form and was ascribed to Moses.[5] Because of the narrative chronology of the books of the Torah—from creation to the death of Moses—their order never varies; the same is true of the Former Prophets, which continue the narrative from the death of Moses to the sixth century BCE. The order of the Latter Prophets is less stable. In most manuscripts, the three longest books, Isaiah, Jeremiah, and Ezekiel, usually occur in that order, which is chronological, but the order of the Minor Prophets in the Book of the Twelve varies

Table 1.1 Tanak(h) (The Jewish Bible)

Torah
    Genesis
    Exodus
    Leviticus
    Numbers
    Deuteronomy

Neviim (*The Prophets*)
    The Former Prophets
        Joshua
        Judges
        1–2 Samuel
        1–2 Kings
    The Latter Prophets
        Isaiah
        Jeremiah
        Ezekiel
        THE BOOK OF THE TWELVE
            Hosea
            Joel
            Amos
            Obadiah
            Jonah
            Micah
            Nahum
            Habakkuk
            Zephaniah
            Haggai
            Zechariah
            Malachi

Ketuvim (*The Writings*)
    Psalms
    Proverbs
    Job
    The Five Scrolls
        The Song of Songs
        Ruth
        Lamentations
        Ecclesiastes
        Esther
    Daniel
    Ezra-Nehemiah
    1–2 Chronicles

considerably. There is even more variation in the order of the books in the Writings, which was the last part of the canon to be considered authoritative scripture.

Not all groups within Judaism of the late Second Temple Period (first century BCE to first century CE) agreed about the contents of the canon. The Samaritans considered only the Torah to be scripture. Other Jewish communities included in their canon books that religious authorities eventually rejected; for example, the Essenes at Qumran, a Jewish sect whose library was the Dead Sea Scrolls, seem to have considered the book of *Jubilees* as scripture, but perhaps not the book of Esther. It is clear, however, that the canon was largely established by the end of the first century CE; different groups included other books, and the status of a few books was debated, but by the second century those debates were essentially over in mainstream Judaism.

What are the Apocrypha?

Several other important Jewish religious writings were eventually omitted from the developing canon. These books became known as the Apocrypha, a word meaning "hidden (books)," although there was never anything hidden about them;[6] sometimes they are also called the deuterocanonical ("belonging to a second canon") books. The word "apocryphal," meaning "of doubtful authenticity," comes from the name of this group of books, but despite the word's connotations, these are authentic Jewish religious texts.

Some of the Apocrypha were originally written in Hebrew or Aramaic, but for the most part they were preserved in Greek. They include many genres. We find historical fiction in the books of Tobit and Judith; narrative history in the books of the Maccabees; wisdom literature in the Wisdom of Solomon and Sirach (also known as Ecclesiasticus); and additions to and revision of earlier biblical works, such as 1 Esdras, the Additions to Esther, and the Additions to Daniel. They were written from about the second century BCE to the first century CE.

Fragments of several of the Apocrypha have been identified among the Dead Sea Scrolls, which were part of the library of the Essenes at Qumran, and many are alluded to in the New Testament, suggesting that for some Jewish groups, including early Christians, they may have been considered canonical scripture. Yet, although some of the Apocrypha continued to be quoted by rabbis and to be part of a kind of secondary canon in Jewish tradition, they were ultimately not included in the Tanakh because of their late date, or because they had not been written in the sacred languages of Hebrew or Aramaic.

What are the Pseudepigrapha?

"Pseudepigrapha" is a term used by scholars for some of the many Jewish writings from the third century BCE to well into the Common Era that are generally not considered authoritative scripture.[7] The word "pseudepigrapha" means "falsely attributed works," because many of the Pseudepigrapha are attributed to major biblical characters, none of whom can plausibly be identified as their authors. Among the Pseudepigrapha are works such as "testaments," purported last words of such characters as Adam, Abraham, Isaac, Jacob, Moses, and Job; apocalypses, recounting revelations concerning the end of the world made to Adam, Elijah, and others; expansions of biblical narratives such as *Joseph and Aseneth* (see Genesis 41:50), *Jubilees*, and the *Martyrdom and Ascension of Isaiah*; and hymns, prayers, and wisdom literature attributed to various individuals.[8]

Some Pseudepigrapha, such as *Jubilees* and *1 Enoch*, are found among the Dead Sea Scrolls, suggesting that for the Essenes at least they may have been canonical. New Testament writers also sometimes quote or allude to some of the Pseudepigrapha as if they were canonical. For example, Jude 14–15 quotes *1*

Enoch 1.9, and Jude 9 describes a conflict between the arch-angel Michael and the devil about Moses's body, probably a reference to a now-lost ending of the *Testament of Moses*.

What is the Bible in Christianity?

By the early second century CE, Jews had reached agreement on which books were their scriptures. In Christianity the situation was and continues to be more complicated. The earliest Christians were Jews, and their scriptures were thus the same as those of other Jews. The versions, or editions, of those scriptures that the earliest Christian writers used, however, did not always correspond to what became the traditional text of the Hebrew Bible, the Masoretic Text (see pages 19–20). Writing in Greek, the authors of the books that eventually became the New Testament, and most other early Christian writers as well, usually quoted the Septuagint, the Greek translation and edition of the Tanakh, made beginning in the third century BCE. For most books this Greek edition corresponds to the Masoretic Text, but there are some important differences, especially in books such as Jeremiah, Job, Daniel, and Esther. The Septuagint also eventually included the Apocrypha, which thus became part of the developing Christian canon.

By the fourth century CE, Christians had rearranged the books of the Jewish scriptures. First came all the books identified as historical—those dealing with the past. So, to the Torah (in Greek, the Pentateuch) and the Former Prophets of the Tanakh were added the books of Ruth, Chronicles, Ezra and Nehemiah (now separated into two books), and Esther, along with some of the Apocrypha—Tobit, Judith, and 1 and 2 Maccabees. The second division of the Christian canon contains what are often called poetical and wisdom books, which can be viewed as having to do with life and worship in the present. Included in this division are Job, Psalms, Proverbs, Ecclesiastes, the Song of Solomon, and, from the Apocrypha, the Wisdom of Solomon and Sirach. Last come the Latter

Prophets of the Tanakh, understood as dealing with the future and strategically placed just before the New Testament, whose events they were believed to predict. After the book of Jeremiah was placed the book of Lamentations, because he was thought to be its author, and, from the Apocrypha, the book of Baruch, attributed to the prophet Jeremiah's scribe, and The Letter of Jeremiah. The book of Daniel was placed after Ezekiel, because Daniel was also identified as a prophet.[9]

What is the New Testament?

Some of the growing body of early Christian literature also came to be considered authoritative, so Christians developed a major addition to the Jewish scriptures: the New Testament. For most denominations, it has twenty-seven canonical books: four Gospels; Acts of Apostles, a narrative about the development of Christianity after the death of Jesus; twenty-one letters by or at least attributed to important early Christian leaders; and the book of Revelation, an account of the end times.

There were debates about including some of these books in the canon, such as James, Jude, and 3 John, and about some that were ultimately not included, such as several Gospels other than Matthew, Mark, Luke, and John; several other Acts of individual apostles as well as letters purporting to be by some of them; an apocalyptic work, *Shepherd of Hermas*; and the *Didache* ("teaching"; the opening lines of the work give its full title: "The teaching of the Lord by the twelve apostles to the nations"), a late first-century or early second-century manual of Christian belief and practice.

The books of the New Testament were written over a much shorter period than those of the Hebrew Bible and the Apocrypha. Scholars agree that the earliest are some of the letters of Paul, written in the late 40s and 50s CE, and the latest is 2 Peter, written no later than 150 CE. So, the books that eventually made up the New Testament were all written within a century or so after the death of Jesus, which occurred about 30 CE.

The two parts of the Christian Bible are familiarly known as the Old Testament (an archaic rendering of "old covenant") and the New Testament ("new covenant"), terminology used at least since the late second century and based on Jeremiah 31:31 and Hebrews 8:8–13. Many modern scholars prefer not to use the term "Old Testament" because it is implicitly derogatory toward Judaism, and use "Hebrew Bible" instead. (See Table 1.2.)

Table 1.2 Christian Bibles

Old Testament

Greek Orthodox[10]	Roman Catholic	Protestants
(Historical Books)		
Genesis	Genesis	Genesis
Exodus	Exodus	Exodus
Leviticus	Leviticus	Leviticus
Numbers	Numbers	Numbers
Deuteronomy	Deuteronomy	Deuteronomy
Joshua	Joshua	Joshua
Judges	Judges	Judges
Ruth	Ruth	Ruth
1–2 Samuel	1–2 Samuel	1–2 Samuel
1–2 Kings	1–2 Kings	1–2 Kings
1–2 Chronicles	1–2 Chronicles	1–2 Chronicles
1 Esdras		
Ezra	Ezra	Ezra
Nehemiah	Nehemiah	Nehemiah
Tobit	Tobit	
Judith	Judith	
Esther	Esther	Esther
Additions to Esther	Additions to Esther	
1 Maccabees	1 Maccabees	
2 Maccabees	2 Maccabees	
3 Maccabees		

(*continued*)

Table 1.2 Continued

(Poetical Books)		
Job	Job	Job
Psalms (including Psalm 151)	Psalms	Psalms
Prayer of Manasseh		
Proverbs	Proverbs	Proverbs
Ecclesiastes	Ecclesiastes	Ecclesiastes
Song of Songs	Song of Songs	Song of Songs
Wisdom	Wisdom	
Sirach	Sirach	
(Prophetic Books)		
Isaiah	Isaiah	Isaiah
Jeremiah	Jeremiah	Jeremiah
Lamentations	Lamentations	Lamentations
Baruch	Baruch (including Letter of Jeremiah)	
Letter of Jeremiah		
Ezekiel	Ezekiel	Ezekiel
Daniel	Daniel	Daniel
Additions to Daniel	Additions to Daniel	
Hosea	Hosea	Hosea
Joel	Joel	Joel
Amos	Amos	Amos
Obadiah	Obadiah	Obadiah
Jonah	Jonah	Jonah
Micah	Micah	Micah
Nahum	Nahum	Nahum
Habakkuk	Habakkuk	Habakkuk
Zephaniah	Zephaniah	Zephaniah
Haggai	Haggai	Haggai
Zechariah	Zechariah	Zechariah
Malachi	Malachi	Malachi
4 Maccabees		

Table 1.2   Continued

New Testament

(Gospels)
    Matthew
    Mark
    Luke
    John

    Acts of Apostles

(Letters or Epistles)
    Romans
    1 Corinthians
    2 Corinthians
    Galatians
    Ephesians
    Philippians
    Colossians
    1 Thessalonians
    2 Thessalonians
    1 Timothy
    2 Timothy
    Titus
    Philemon
    Hebrews
    James
    1 Peter
    2 Peter
    1 John
    2 John
    3 John
    Jude

    Revelation

Why is the Protestant Old Testament different from that of Roman Catholics and Eastern Orthodox Christians?

Because of Martin Luther. In his classic translation of the Bible into German, completed in 1534, Luther placed the books known as the Apocrypha after the Old Testament, as a kind of appendix, stating that these "books, while not having the same authority as sacred scripture, are still useful and good to read."[11] He did so for two reasons. First, they were, as far as he knew, written in Greek rather than in Hebrew or Aramaic, and were therefore in his view less authentic. Second, several passages in them seemed to support Roman Catholic doctrines that he had rejected, such as purgatory and the importance of good works.[12]

The result is that the Protestant canon of the Old Testament and the Jewish canon, the Tanakh, have the same books, but in a somewhat different order. And, while traditionally the Jewish canon has twenty-four books, the Protestant canon has thirty-nine, counting Samuel, Kings, and Chronicles as two books each, Ezra and Nehemiah as separate books, and each of the Minor Prophets as a separate book.

However, many modern Protestant study Bibles do include the Apocrypha, in a separate section between the Old Testament and the New Testament.

2

LANGUAGES, TEXTS, AND TRANSLATIONS

What languages was the Bible written in?

The Bible was written in three languages. The first is Hebrew, which was the primary language of the ancient Israelites for most of the biblical period, until Aramaic gradually replaced it. Hebrew continued to be used by Jews for scholarship and in worship, so that its status became something like that of Latin in the Roman Catholic Church. In a remarkable revival in the late nineteenth century, however, Hebrew became the preferred language of Jews who had immigrated to the Promised Land in Ottoman Palestine, and since then it has become a complex living language, spoken not only by Israelis but by many Jews worldwide.[1] Almost all of the Hebrew Bible is in Hebrew, and many of the Apocrypha were also originally written in Hebrew.

Aramaic, a Semitic language closely related to Hebrew, was originally the language of several kingdoms in Aram, roughly the same as modern Syria. Those kingdoms were conquered by the Assyrians from northern Mesopotamia in the ninth and eighth centuries BCE, and Aramaic became the lingua franca of the Assyrian Empire and its successor, the Persian Empire; Aramaic texts have been found as far east as Afghanistan and Pakistan, and as far west as Greece. In what had been the kingdoms of Israel and Judah, Aramaic gradually replaced Hebrew as the dominant spoken language; in the Gospels, Jesus is quoted as using Aramaic on several occasions.[2] In the Hebrew Bible, Ezra 4:8–6:18 and Daniel 2:4b–7:28 are in Aramaic, as are Jeremiah 10:11 and two words in Genesis 31:47 (quoting Jacob's Aramean uncle Laban); the presence of these Aramaic parts is why the frequently used term "Hebrew Bible" is not entirely accurate. Several of the Apocrypha were probably originally written in Aramaic as well.

When the Greeks under Alexander the Great took over the Near East in the late fourth century BCE, Greek became the preferred language of the educated elite in the Near East, and remained so even after the Romans took over the region in the first century BCE. Several of the books of the Apocrypha were written in Greek, as was the entire New Testament. Even Paul's letter to the Romans was written in Greek; every educated Roman at that time was fluent in Greek.

In addition to these three primary languages, there are occasional words in the Bible borrowed from other languages. Because the Persians, from what is now modern Iran, controlled much of the ancient Near East from the mid-sixth to the late fourth centuries BCE, we find Persian words like "paradise," meaning an enclosed garden, and "satrap," a Persian official. In the later books of the Hebrew Bible there are also a few Greek words, and in the New Testament, which was written in Greek, a few originally Latin words, reflecting Roman control of the eastern Mediterranean lands.

For more than two thousand years, as more and more of its books became authoritative scripture, the Bible has been translated into the languages of people who did not know Hebrew and Aramaic, and, eventually, for the Apocrypha and the New Testament, of people who did not know Greek.

How many translations of the Bible are there?

Since antiquity, the entire Bible has been translated into hundreds of languages. Some parts, especially the book of Psalms and the New Testament, have been translated into several thousand more. That work continues, under the auspices of such groups as the United Bible Societies and the Wycliffe Bible Translators, which have also made significant contributions to the discipline of linguistics in the course of their work.

What are the oldest translations of the Bible?

The earliest translation of the Hebrew Bible was into Greek. It was produced in the third and second centuries BCE for Jews living in Egypt and in other Greek-speaking regions in the eastern Mediterranean who no longer understood the original Hebrew. It is called the Septuagint, from the Greek word for "seventy," so scholars often refer to it by the abbreviation "LXX."

So important was this translation that legends developed about how it was made. A second-century BCE source, the *Letter of Aristeas*, reports that the king of Egypt, Ptolemy II (ruled 285–246), was collecting books for the royal library in Alexandria, his capital city. At the king's suggestion, his acquisitions librarian wrote to the high priest in Jerusalem, asking him to send seventy-two scholars (six from each of the twelve tribes of Israel) to Alexandria to translate the Torah into Greek. The seventy-two scholars produced an accurate translation in seventy-two days—according to a later source, so accurate that although the translators worked independently, they produced identical versions, which could have happened only by divine inspiration.[3] The Greek translation of the Torah was thus as authoritative as the original Hebrew. The rest of the Hebrew Bible was translated subsequently, along with other Jewish writings, and the Septuagint became the primary version of the Bible used by Greek-speaking Jews, including the writers of the New Testament. Its use by Jews declined, however, as Christians adopted the Septuagint as their primary text of the Old Testament. For Orthodox Christians the Septuagint continues to be the authoritative version of the Old Testament.

By the second century BCE, translations of the Hebrew Bible into Aramaic were also being made. Known as "Targums" (which means "translations"), these became the standard translations used by many Jews beginning early in the Common Era, especially in Palestine and Babylonia. Related to the Targums is the Peshitta, a translation of the Jewish scriptures and of the New Testament into Syriac, an Aramaic dialect, dating to the second century CE.

Another very important ancient translation is the Vulgate. Completed in 405 CE, it was a translation of the Hebrew Bible, the Apocrypha, and the New Testament into Latin by the great scholar Jerome. The Vulgate became the principal text of the Bible for the Roman Catholic Church and is still used in official Vatican documents.

How do translators work?

Beginning with the Septuagint, most translations have been made by committees. Scholars usually divide up the books to be translated, and then the different versions are edited for consistency of approach and style. Translations of the entire Bible by individuals are less frequent. Notable examples are Jerome and Martin Luther; in the modern period James Moffat, Franz Rosenzweig and Martin Buber, and Edgar J. Goodspeed; and, more recently, Everett Fox, Robert Alter, and John Goldingay.[4] Whether working together or individually, translators have to decide on their approach. The two extremes are literal translation and dynamic equivalence.

What is a literal translation?

A literal translation, often called "formal equivalence," is one that almost on a word-for-word basis attempts to produce a version as close as possible to the original. The biblical languages, especially Hebrew and Aramaic, are very different in structure and in syntax from English—for example, the opening of Psalm 23, "The LORD is my shepherd, I shall not want" has only four words in Hebrew. Another issue is style; for example, Ephesians 1:3–14 is a single, very long sentence in the original Greek, but few translators have tried to reproduce this precisely.[5]

Moreover, an overly literal translation can result in some awkwardness. Here are two recent literal translations of the first three verses of the book of Genesis:

> At the beginning of God's creating of the heavens
>   and the earth,
> when the earth was wild and waste,
> darkness over the face of Ocean, rushing spirit of
>   God hovering over the face of the waters—
> God said: Let there be light! And there was light.[6]

> When God began to create heaven and earth, and
>   the earth then was welter and waste and darkness
>   over the deep and God's breath hovering over the
>   waters, God said, "Let there be light." And there
>   was light.[7]

Both have the advantage of making the familiar seem fresh, but neither to my mind is exactly elegant English, even though the original is elegant Hebrew.

A literal translation can have advantages. For example, the Hebrew verb meaning "to know" does refer to what we might call intellectual knowledge and understanding. Sometimes, however, it is used as euphemism for sexual intercourse—"to know in the biblical sense." So, we are told that after they had been expelled from the garden of Eden, "Adam knew his wife Eve, and she became pregnant, and gave birth to Cain" (Genesis 4:1). Literal translations use the English verb "to know" in this verse; less literal translations interpret it, correctly, as "had intercourse with."[8] But such a translation means that readers may miss this nuance of the verb elsewhere, as when, speaking through the prophet Amos, God says to Israel, "You only have I known of all the nations of the earth" (Amos 3:2), alluding to the frequent metaphor of Israel as the deity's wife.

What is dynamic equivalence?

At the other end of the translation spectrum is dynamic equivalence (also referred to as "functional equivalence"), which attempts to express the meaning of the original text in the target language. At its most extreme, this amounts to paraphrase, as in the rendering in the Contemporary English Version of Genesis 4:1 (see above) as "Adam and Eve had a son." Sometimes, too, a dynamic-equivalence translation will substitute a culturally appropriate sense for the actual meaning, by, for example, rendering the phrase "white as snow" (Daniel 7:9) as "white as egret feathers" or "very, very white" in a translation for a culture that has no direct experience of snow.[9]

What is textual criticism?

Another issue facing translators is what exactly to translate. As is true for most ancient literature, we no longer have the original works that the biblical writers and editors produced. Rather, what we have are copies of copies of copies, most of which date centuries after the works themselves were written. All of these copies are manuscripts, painstakingly copied by hand by scribes over the ages, until the invention of movable type by Johannes Gutenberg in the mid-fifteenth century. The first complete book printed by Gutenberg was the Bible, in the Vulgate translation.

Generally, scribes intended to copy exactly what was in front of them, but unsurprisingly at times they made mistakes: confusing two letters, skipping a line, and the like. More rarely, scribes deliberately changed the text they were copying, either to correct an earlier scribe's mistake or because they thought the text was in error theologically or in other ways.[10] So, no

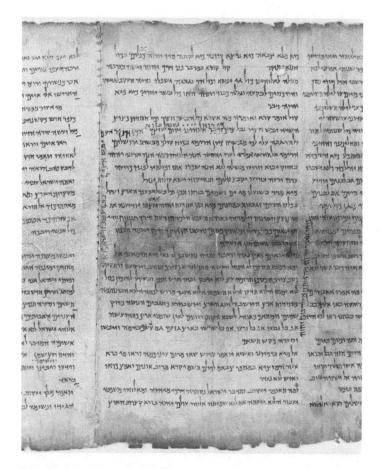

Figure 2.1 A column of the Great Isaiah Scroll from Qumran, which dates to the second century BCE, showing scribal corrections. The passage shown is Isaiah 40:2–28.

Photo © The Israel Museum, Jerusalem by Ardon Bar-Hama

single manuscript is entirely reliable. Rather, scholars need to compare different manuscripts and decide which readings of every verse are probably closest to the original. That is called textual criticism.

For the Hebrew Bible, the oldest complete manuscripts of the Masoretic ("traditional") Text (often abbreviated MT) date to the Middle Ages; even the earliest of these, the Aleppo

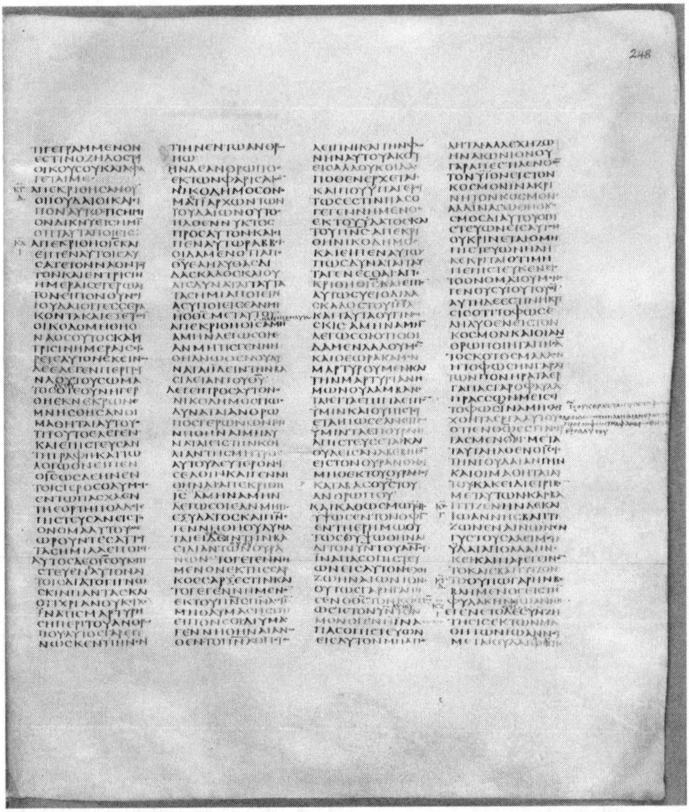

Figure 2.2 A page of the Greek manuscript Codex Sinaiticus, which dates to the fourth century CE, showing scribal corrections. The passage shown is John 2:17–3:35.

British Library/Granger

Codex and the Leningrad Codex, from the tenth and eleventh centuries respectively, are not identical in every respect. In the mid-twentieth century, however, a trove of hundreds of biblical and other texts was discovered near the Dead Sea. Known as the Dead Sea Scrolls, they include manuscripts of every book of the Hebrew Bible except Esther (perhaps a coincidence), almost all of which are fragmentary. (See Figure 2.1.)

The Dead Sea Scrolls and the later manuscripts largely agree, showing how careful scribes were over the centuries. But occasionally there are differences. Following the Masoretic Text, the translation of Deuteronomy 32:8 in the New International Version (NIV) reads:

> When the Most High gave the nations their inheritance,
>   when he divided all mankind,
> he set up boundaries for the peoples
>   according to the number of the sons of Israel.

According to this verse, when the Most High God was determining how many different nations there would be, he decided that there would be twelve, just as there were twelve tribes of Israel.

But like some other translations, for the phrase "sons of Israel" the NIV has a textual note, which reads: "Masoretic Text: Dead Sea Scrolls (see also Septuagint) *sons of God.*" The translators are letting us know that they are translating the medieval Masoretic Text, but also that both in the Dead Sea Scrolls and in the ancient translation into Greek known as the Septuagint the text says "sons of God." Many other translations, especially the more recent, use the alternate reading. Only one of these readings can be original. It is difficult to explain why a scribe would change "sons of Israel" to "sons of God," but easy to see why a pious scribe would change the text to remove explicit polytheism. So, "sons of God" is the better reading, and is followed by the New Revised Standard Version (NRSV) and some other recent translations.

The oldest complete New Testament manuscripts date from the fourth century CE (see Figure 2.2), although fragmentary manuscripts dating as early as the second century have been found. As with manuscripts of the Hebrew Bible, these New Testament texts do not always agree. Sometimes longer passages are at issue. In the earliest surviving manuscripts, the Gospel of Mark ends with the discovery of Jesus's empty tomb by three women who were his disciples. At the tomb, a young man, probably an angel,[11] tells them that Jesus had been raised from the dead and that they should instruct his other disciples and Peter to meet him in Galilee. But the women "said nothing to anyone, for they were afraid" (16:8). This abrupt ending has puzzled modern scholars, and apparently ancient scribes as well: In later manuscripts, we find two longer, alternate endings, neither of which is likely original. They are made up of snippets from the other Gospels, and were added by scribes to provide what they apparently thought was missing in the manuscript they were copying.

The ending of the "Lord's Prayer" in the Sermon on the Mount in Matthew 6:13 provides another example. Here are the NRSV and the King James Version (KJV):

> And do not bring us to the time of trial, but rescue us from the evil one.

> And lead us not into temptation but deliver us from evil: For thine is the kingdom, and the power, and the glory, for ever. Amen.

Again, the earliest manuscripts do not have the familiar addition in the KJV, which may have been a pious scribe's gloss taken by a subsequent copyist to be part of the original.[12]

Examples like these are not trivial. They show us yet again how complicated it is to define what the Bible actually is. Are the longer endings of Mark and the Lord's Prayer biblical, in the sense of being part of authoritative scripture? Should translators include them or not?

What are some important English translations of the Bible?

Certainly the most important English translation of the Bible is the Authorized Version, published under the patronage of King James I of England in 1611 and thus known as the King

James Version. Compiled by a committee appointed by the king, the translators were contemporaries of Shakespeare, and their work rivals his for its status in English literature. (Luther's translation of the Bible into German has a similar status in German literature.) The KJV rapidly became the primary translation of the Bible for English-speaking Protestants, and still is for many.[13]

Recognizing both that there were errors and inconsistencies in the KJV and that the biblical manuscripts they had translated were not always the best texts, a modest revision was published in England in 1885 as the Revised Version. It deliberately did not change the by-then-archaic style of the KJV, such as the use of "thee" and "thou." Because it was considered too British in tone, scholars in the United States produced their own revision, the American Standard Version, in 1901, and, because the English language is constantly changing, the Revised Standard Version (RSV) in 1952 and the New Revised Standard Version in 1989. Another revision, apparently also somewhat modest, is in the works.

Some American Protestants, however, thought the RSV and especially the NRSV were too liberal theologically, and so a committee of evangelical scholars produced the NIV in 1978. This was revised as Today's NIV in 2005 and 2011 (the latter controversial because of its use of inclusive language). For others, many of these translations were too literal, and more colloquial versions were published, including the Good News Bible (1966–79, revised in 1992) and the Common English Bible (CEB; 2011).

Not surprisingly, Jewish and Roman Catholic groups produced their own translations of the Bible into English. In the United States, the Jewish Publication Society published a complete translation of the Hebrew Bible in 1917,[14] and another in 1985 (NJPS).[15] English Catholic exiles in France produced the Douay-Rheims Bible (New Testament 1582; Old Testament 1609–10), but unlike the KJV it was translated not from the original languages, but from the Vulgate. Revised often, this remained the principal Roman Catholic Bible in English until the mid-twentieth century. Under the auspices of the Confraternity of Christian Doctrine, the bishops of the United States commissioned a new translation, which was published as the New American Bible (NAB; 1970); the committee that produced it included Jewish and Protestant scholars. It was lightly revised in the 1980s and 1990s to use more inclusive and colloquial language; a fully revised edition (NABRE) was published in 2011, and undid some of the earlier revisions.

Should translations of the Bible use inclusive language?

One of the issues that has concerned translators in the last few decades is how to translate gender-specific language in the original texts. The issue is complicated by the differences between Hebrew and English and Greek and English. For example, the Hebrew word *ish* and the Greek word *aner* mean an individual human male,[16] whereas Hebrew *adam* and Greek *anthropos* are usually collective terms for the human species. Both, however, were usually translated into English as "man." Thus, *adam* is used in Deuteronomy 8:3, and in its quotation in Matthew 4:4 *anthropos* is used; these verses are rendered by the KJV as "man doth not live by bread only" and "man shall not live by bread alone." The NRSV, avoiding the apparently objectionable "man," translates "one does not live by bread alone," and the CEB has "people don't live on bread alone." Such translations are arguably closer to the sense of the original.

Also, what was not gender-specific in Greek could be made so in English. In John 15:13, the KJV has "Greater love hath no man than this, that a man lay down his life for his friends," but the opening words in Greek literally mean "greater love than this no one has," so translators wishing to be inclusive have justification in the original.

Sometimes, too, the use of inclusive language can be problematic. Note the difference in these translations of the opening words of Psalm 1:

Blessed is the man who does not walk in the counsel of the wicked.

Happy are those who do not follow the counsel of the wicked.

The first translation is from the NABRE, published in 2011. One might think that the second, with its more inclusive language, is more recent, but in fact it was from the earlier, partial revision of the NAB, published in 1991. That revision avoided gender-specific language both about human beings and about God, and was banned from liturgical use by the Vatican. The newer translation is thus a reversion to a less inclusive style of translation, but it is also a more literal rendering of the original.

Similarly, although in his letters Paul frequently addresses his correspondents as "brothers," inclusive translations often render this "brothers and sisters," adding words that are not in the original Greek. There is no escaping the fact that the worldview of the biblical writers was patriarchal. Should translators deliberately obscure this? Or perhaps two types of translation should be made: one that renders as accurately as possible what the original language says, and another that uses more inclusive language and thus is more suitable for liturgical contexts.

Why is translation so difficult?

One reason is that translation involves interpretation, and the correct interpretation is not always clear. Probably the most controversial translation issue in the Hebrew Bible concerns Isaiah 7:14. The KJV has this: "Behold, a virgin shall conceive, and bear a son, and shall call his name Immanuel." But that is not really what the Hebrew says; the CEB is more accurate: "The young woman is pregnant and is about to give birth to a son, and she will name him Immanuel." In its context the verse is describing an already pregnant woman whose sexual history is not relevant. Why then did most translators of the Bible, especially Christian translators, until modern times think that it referred to some woman in the future, who was a virgin? Because the verse is quoted in the Gospel of Matthew, in the context of Joseph's dream informing him that his fiancée was "with child from the Holy Spirit":

> All this took place to fulfill what had been spoken by the Lord through the prophet: "Look, the virgin shall conceive and bear a son, and they shall name him Emmanuel." (Matthew 1:18, 22–23, NRSV)

Does Matthew's interpretation, based on the Septuagint,[17] override for Christians the plain sense of the original Hebrew? Or is Matthew's interpretation to be understood in the context of his belief that the Old Testament in general, and especially the prophets, were in fact divinely given predictions about Jesus?

Here is another example of a translation issue that affects theology. Several times in his letters Paul uses the Greek phrase *pistis (Iesou) Christou*, which can be translated in two ways: "faith in (Jesus) Christ" and "the faith of (Jesus) Christ."[18] The first translation refers to the faith of believers in Christ, whereas the second refers to Christ's own faithfulness. Note the difference in two translations of Galatians 2:16:

> We know that a person is justified not by the works of the law but through faith in Jesus Christ. (NRSV)

We know that a person isn't made righteous by the works of the Law but rather through the faithfulness of Jesus Christ. (CEB)

Are believers "justified" by their own faith, or because of Christ's obedience even unto death? Or is the ambiguity perhaps deliberate? Translators must choose one meaning, so that readers of the Bible using only one translation will be unaware of the issue.

These examples illustrate why I advise my students to consult several different translations when they are looking closely at a biblical text. This enables them to get closer to the meaning(s) of the original and to identify issues of interpretation. In this book I will use various translations of the Bible, so that readers can get a sense of the differences among them.

3

THE CONTENTS OF THE BIBLE

What are the books of the Bible?

The Bible is divided into books. For easy reference, scholars in the Middle Ages divided the books into chapters (except for the very short books), and beginning in the fifteenth century the chapters into verses, just as study editions of Shakespeare's plays have not only acts and scenes, but also line numbers. So, for example, the book of Genesis has fifty chapters, and each chapter has its own verse numbers; thus, Genesis 6:4 refers to the fourth verse of the sixth chapter of the book; Genesis 7:5 refers to the fifth verse of the seventh chapter. Because Jewish scholars and Christian scholars used slightly different systems, chapter and verse numbers in Jewish and Christian Bibles are not always the same.[1]

The books of the Bible vary considerably in length. The book with the most chapters is Psalms, which has 150, and it also has the most verses (over 2,400), although in terms of word count both Jeremiah and Genesis are longer. Psalms also has the shortest and longest chapters in the Bible, 117 (2 verses) and 119 (176 verses). Several books of the Bible consist of only one chapter, including Obadiah in the Hebrew Bible, the Prayer of Manasseh in the Apocrypha, and Philemon, 2 and 3 John, and Jude in the New Testament. Obadiah is the shortest book in the Hebrew Bible, and 2 and 3 John are the shortest books in the New Testament.

How were the books of the Bible named?

Like many other ancient books, most books of the Bible did not originally have titles. The familiar titles of almost all biblical books were added later, as they were copied, collected, and catalogued. Most of these names are derived either from the contents of the books or from their opening words (often also the case for other books of antiquity), or identify their supposed author.

The English (and originally the ancient Greek) names of the first five books of the Bible, the Torah or Pentateuch, describe their general contents: Genesis describes beginnings and births; Exodus recounts the Hebrews' escape from Egypt under Moses's leadership; Numbers features two censuses; Leviticus, named for the priestly tribe of Levi, contains many ritual prescriptions; and Deuteronomy (from Greek, meaning "second law") is a collection of laws, many of which occur earlier in the Pentateuch. The books of Joshua and Judges are named for their principal characters. The books known as 1 and 2 Samuel were originally one book, and were named for the prophet Samuel, who is a principal character, especially in the opening chapters. The books of 1 and 2 Kings were also originally one book, and cover the period of the kings of Israel and Judah.[2] Other books named for their principal characters are Ezra, Nehemiah, Esther, Job, and Ruth. The books of the prophets are named for their presumed authors, as are the Song of Solomon and Ecclesiastes. Finally, the books of Chronicles, Psalms, Proverbs, and Lamentations are named for their contents.

In Jewish tradition, some books get their names from an opening word or a prominent word at the book's beginning. Thus, in Hebrew the books of the Torah are called *Bereshit* ("in the beginning"), *Shemot* ("names"), *Vayikra* ("and [the LORD] called"), *Bemidbar* ("in the wilderness"), and *Devarim* ("words"), and Lamentations is named *Ekhah* ("how"). Also, the book of Ecclesiastes is called *Qohelet* (also "Koheleth"), the Hebrew name or epithet of its pseudonymous author in 1:1.

The books of the Apocrypha have similarly transparent titles, except for the alternate Latin title Ecclesiasticus ("belonging to the church"; not to be confused with Ecclesiastes) for Sirach, which has as its full title "The Wisdom of Jesus, Son of Sirach," often also abbreviated to "Ben Sira" (the Hebrew form).

In the New Testament, the four Gospels are named for their presumed authors, as are the letters of James, Peter, John, and Jude. The letters attributed to Paul include in their titles both his name and the individual or group to whom the letters are addressed. The title Acts of Apostles describes that book's content, as does the full title of the last book of the New Testament, "The Revelation to John." The letter to the Hebrews, although it alludes to the apostle Paul in its concluding verses, is not explicitly attributed to him, and is probably named for its presumed audience of Jewish Christians.

Why is genre important?

Like other anthologies, the Bible contains a variety of genres. Some of its books are narrative history, some are historical fiction; some are poetry, some are prose; some are letters, and some are prayers. Identifying genre is an important aspect of interpretation, because genre affects meaning. For example, we need to distinguish between narrative history and historical fiction, between myth, legend, and history, between reporting and satire. So, as we read the Bible, we need to identify genres carefully, because that will help us better understand what the biblical writers' messages were.

What are the principal genres in the Hebrew Bible/Old Testament?

The principal genres in the Hebrew Bible/Old Testament are narrative history and historical fiction, myths, laws, hymns and prayers, wisdom literature, proverbs, prophetic literature, and apocalyptic literature. But they overlap frequently: We find narrative history in some prophetic literature and in hymns; prophetic material in narrative history, in historical fiction, and in hymns; and so on. Within many books we also find many different genres.

Which books of the Hebrew Bible/Old Testament are narrative history?

A narrative history is a chronologically ordered account of persons and events. But in ancient narrative histories neither all of the characters nor all of the events described are necessarily historical in the sense that they actually existed or took place. In the Hebrew Bible, the books of Genesis through 2 Kings form one continuous narrative history, from the creation of the world to the fall of Jerusalem to the Babylonians in 586 BCE. That narrative provides a framework into which different writers over several centuries inserted all sorts of genres, including genealogies, itineraries, speeches, poems, and laws.

Genesis moves briskly from creation to the stories of the Garden of Eden, the Flood, and the Tower of Babel, and then slows down to focus on four generations of one extended family, beginning with Abraham, his wives Sarah and Hagar, and their sons Isaac and Ishmael. There follows a relatively short account of the life of Isaac, his wife Rebekah, and their twin sons Esau and Jacob, and then moves to the story of Jacob and his wives and children. At the end of Genesis, that family, some seventy persons in all we are told, has ended up in Egypt.

The books of Exodus through Deuteronomy narrow the focus still further. Exodus begins with the birth of Moses, who will liberate his kin, the Israelites, the descendants of Jacob, from Egyptian slavery and lead them to the border of the Promised Land. During that journey, God gives Moses and the Israelites many instructions about how they are to live and how they are to worship him. Deuteronomy ends with the death and burial of Moses.

The narrative of the Former Prophets continues the chronological sequence, giving a history of the Israelites in the Promised Land. The book of Joshua recounts how the Israelites conquered that land under the leadership of Moses's divinely designated successor Joshua. The book of Judges describes how they fared there under the leadership of individuals called "judges," local leaders appointed by God in times of crisis. In 1 Samuel, the Israelites adopt a monarchical form of government, and the rest of the books of Samuel and Kings describes the history of Israel under the leadership of kings, first as a united monarchy under David and his son Solomon, and then as two divided kingdoms, Israel in the north until its capture by the Assyrians in the late eighth century BCE, and Judah in the south until its capture by the Babylonians in the early sixth century BCE.

Using the already-existing narrative of Genesis–2 Kings as the principal source, the author of 1 and 2 Chronicles presents another narrative history, covering roughly the same time frame. This writer begins with the genealogy of the first human, Adam, and concludes with a decree of the Persian king Cyrus the Great in 538 BCE allowing those Judeans who had been exiled to Babylonia to return to their homeland. The books of Ezra and Nehemiah, probably originally a single work, continue this narrative into the fifth century BCE, with some gaps.

In the Apocrypha, 1 and 2 Maccabees are also narrative histories, two separate accounts of the revolt of the Maccabees against religious persecution by Greek rulers in the early second century BCE in Judea (as Judah had come to be called).

Which books of the Hebrew Bible/Old Testament are historical fiction?

Scholars have identified several books in the Writings and the Apocrypha as historical fiction, narratives set in historical contexts but describing individuals and events that are often not historical. All of these books are relatively brief. Ruth and Jonah are essentially short stories, the first about King David's great-grandmother Ruth, and the second about the prophet Jonah, mentioned briefly in 2 Kings 14:25, and his mission to the Assyrian capital of Nineveh. The books of Tobit, Esther, and Judith are novellas, named for their principal characters and set in Assyria, Persia, and Judea, respectively. Chapters 1– 6 of the book of Daniel are a series of tales about Judean exiles in Babylon and Persia, including Daniel in the lions' den, as are two of the Additions to the book of Daniel: Susanna, and Bel and the Dragon. The book of 3 Maccabees, an account of royal persecution of Jews in Egypt in the late third century BCE, also belongs to this category.

These books are characterized as historical fiction because their history and geography are often confused; because they contain invented dialogue between characters, some of whom are angels; and because they usually feature heroes who model faithfulness to their ancestral Israelite religion under foreign rule. For example, the book of Jonah calls the Assyrian ruler "the king of Nineveh," but that was never his title. Add to that folkloric elements such as Jonah sleeping through a terrible storm at sea, living in the belly of a big fish (not a whale!) for three days and three nights, and a magic plant, and it is clear that this is fiction. The book of Judith opens with a series of errors, perhaps signaling to the reader that it not to be understood as a historically accurate narrative: "It was the twelfth year of the reign of Nebuchadnezzar who ruled over the Assyrians in the great city of Nineveh." But Nebuchadnezzar was king of the Babylonians, not the Assyrians; the twelfth year of his reign was 593 BCE, but Nineveh had been destroyed in 612 BCE. Again, this is not history, but fiction. Finally, in the book of Tobit, in addition to its confused chronology, the plot includes Job-like disasters to its principal character; an attacking fish; magic potions; and a demon who killed in succession seven of a woman's husbands on their wedding nights.

Does the Bible contain myths?

Simply defined, a myth is a story in which one or more of the principal characters are divine. Writ large, the Bible is certainly a myth: Its principal character is God himself. In its pages he often resembles other gods: He is not just loving and merciful, but capricious, jealous, and sometimes drunk—in short, like other gods and goddesses, he is all too human.

The biblical writers often borrowed and adapted myths from neighboring cultures. We find this especially in the accounts of creation and the Flood in the opening chapters of Genesis. But mythology pervades the entire Bible, especially in poetic texts. Let us take creation itself as an example. Creation is sometimes described as the sequel to a cosmic battle in which God defeated the forces of primeval chaos, after which he established an orderly universe.[3] Furthermore, creation was not necessarily a solitary effort: According to the book of Proverbs, God had a female partner, Wisdom personified, who tells us that "when he marked out the foundations of the earth, then I was the craftsman at his side" (Proverbs 8:29–30, New International Version). Finally, when God's work had been done, not only did he rest, but the other gods celebrated his accomplishments.[4] All of these mythological elements, and many others, have parallels in nonbiblical texts.

Where are laws found in the Bible?

Most biblical laws are presented as divine commands given to individuals and groups in ancient Israel throughout its history. Thus, they most frequently occur in the context of narrative history, being given, for example, to Noah, to Abraham, and especially to Moses (and by him to the Israelites) in the Torah. Many of these laws were preexisting collections that were incorporated into the narrative, including the Ten Commandments (Exodus 20:2–17; Deuteronomy 5:6–21), and what modern scholars call the Covenant Code (Exodus 20:22–23:33), the Holiness Code (Leviticus 17–26), and the Deuteronomic Code

(Deuteronomy 12–26). Most of the legal pronouncements in the Prophets and in the Writings as well as in the Apocrypha are derived from these Pentateuchal collections.

The laws fall into two basic categories. The first is what we would call civil and criminal law: laws having to do with property, marriage, inheritance, violence against persons, and the like. Many of these laws have close parallels in ancient nonbiblical legal collections. It should be noted, however, that since civil and criminal laws are divinely given, they also have a religious dimension, in the sense that breaking them is disobedience to divine commands. The second category is explicitly religious law: how (and how not) to worship, maintain religious purity, practice circumcision, observe the Sabbath, and the like. These laws are more distinctively Israelite.

Many of the laws are also quoted, expanded, and revised in the New Testament, for example in the Sermon on the Mount (Matthew 5–7) and in the "household codes" of some letters, such as Ephesians 5:22–6:9, Colossians 3:18–4:1, and 1 Peter 2:18–3:7. The household codes in particular also have parallels in Greek and Roman literature.

Where are hymns and prayers found in the Bible?

Almost everywhere. Many characters in narrative history and historical fiction frequently pray to God in both prose and poetry. Prayers are also attributed to many of the prophets, and hymns and fragments of hymns appear in the Gospel of Luke, in many of the letters of the New Testament, and in the book of Revelation.

The most important collection of hymns and prayers in the Bible is the book of Psalms, called in Hebrew *Tehillim*, which means "praises." In it we find addresses to God from individuals, including kings, and from the community, asking God for help and thanking him for help given. The book of Psalms also has hymns that were used liturgically, hymns praising God as creator and king, and hymns celebrating divine actions in Israel's history.

The book of Psalms is itself an anthology within the larger anthology that is the Bible. It is a compilation of collections of hymns probably used at various shrines in ancient Israel, and especially in the Temple in Jerusalem, that were combined into a more-or-less final form by the second century BCE. This is clear from repetition within the book: thus, Psalm 14 is virtually identical to Psalm 53, and Psalm 108 combines Psalms 57:7–11 and 60:5–12. It is also clear from the clustering of psalms attributed to several individuals, including not only David and Solomon (see pages 48–51) but also famous priests, such as Asaph and Heman, sons of Korah.[5]

The anonymous ancient editors of the book of Psalms subdivided it into five smaller "books": Psalms 1–41, 42–72, 73–89, 90–106, and 107–150; each of these parts ends with a doxology or blessing. This seems to be a deliberate parallel to the five books of the Torah, implying the special status of the collection.

What is wisdom literature?

Wisdom literature is a term used by modern scholars to describe several genres used in the Bible and elsewhere in the ancient Near East that have to do with living a good life and the ultimate meaning of life. The genres include proverbs, as in the book of Proverbs; dialogues, like the book of Job; and reflections on the meaning of life, as in Ecclesiastes. The same genres are known from nonbiblical ancient Near Eastern texts. In the Apocrypha, the Wisdom of Solomon and Sirach also belong to the category of wisdom literature.

What are proverbs?

Proverbs are short, pithy prose or poetic sayings that give insight into the human condition. Proverbs are a universal genre, familiar to us in such examples as "Little strokes fell great oaks," "Early to bed and early to rise, makes a man healthy, wealthy, and wise," and "Three may keep a secret, if two of them are dead," from Benjamin Franklin's *Poor Richard's Almanack*. According to the book of Sirach, "The mind of the intelligent appreciates proverbs" (3:29), an aphorism confirmed by the many collections of proverbs known worldwide.

One of the frequent features of proverb collections in the ancient Near East is that of a father addressing his son, or a teacher his student; for example:

> My son, heed the discipline of your father,
> and do not forsake the instruction of your mother.
> (Proverbs 1:8, New Jewish
> Publication Society Translation)

The principal collection of proverbs in the Bible is the book of Proverbs, which, like the book of Psalms, is an anthology. This is clear from headings indicating different collections included in the book:

> The proverbs of Solomon, son of David, king of Israel (1:1)
> The proverbs of Solomon (10:1)
> The words of the wise (22:17)
> These also are by the wise (24:23)
> These are other proverbs of Solomon that the officials of King Hezekiah of Judah copied (25:1)
> The words of Agur son of Jakeh (30:1)
> The words of King Lemuel. An oracle that his mother taught him (31:1).

Also, several proverbs occur in more than one of these collections. The book of Proverbs probably reached its more-or-less final shape in the fifth or fourth century BCE. In the Apocrypha, the book of Sirach is in part also an anthology of proverbs, some of which are taken from the book of Proverbs.

In the book of Proverbs, we find proverbs dealing with all aspects of life, from interpersonal relationships to one's relationship with God. The first collection, chapters 1–9, especially focuses on how to please God by devoting oneself to acquiring wisdom. In several longer poems in the book, Wisdom is often personified as God's female partner who invites a young man to acquire her in order to have a fulfilled life.

Individual proverbs also occur throughout the Bible in many different contexts. Jeremiah and Ezekiel both quote, and reject, a popular proverb: "The parents have eaten sour grapes, and the children's teeth are set on edge" (Jeremiah 31:29–30; Ezekiel 18:2–4), meaning that children suffer divine punishment for the actions of their parents. Proverbs also occur in the New Testament; for example, excoriating Christians who have returned to "the moral filth of this world," the author of 2 Peter quotes two proverbs: "A dog returns to his own vomit," and "A washed sow wallows in the mud" (2:22, Common English Bible)—the first from the book of Proverbs (26:11), and the second probably from the nonbiblical *Book of Ahikar*, whose oldest surviving version dates to the fifth century BCE.

What is prophetic literature?

In its simplest sense, prophetic literature is writings by and about individuals called prophets. The term *prophet*, coming from Greek, means "spokesperson." Prophets were men and women who believed, and whose contemporaries believed, that they had a direct line of communication with the divine. Such individuals are well attested in the ancient Near East outside of ancient Israel. The most common Hebrew terms for prophet mean man of God, seer, and one called, all suggesting a special relationship with the god of Israel.[6]

In the Bible, prophets are most widely found in the prophetic books—the Latter Prophets of the Tanakh. These books, especially the longer ones, contain a large number of different genres, including narrative history, hymns, prayers, proverbs, visions, and especially divine pronouncement of judgment on Israel's enemies, on Israel itself, and on groups and individuals within it. Most of the prophetic books have complicated literary histories.

Prophets are also frequently referred to elsewhere in the Bible. They are especially prominent in the books of Kings, providing as it were a kind of running commentary on their times. Both there, and in the prophetic books, prophets are presented as divinely inspired interpreters of Israel's history: its past, its present, and its future, especially its immediate future. In several prophetic books, especially in the last stages of their formation, and in the chronologically later prophets, we also find predictions of a more distant future. Eventually this will develop into apocalyptic literature.

Prophecy continued to exist in Christianity, as also later in Islam. Both John the Baptist and Jesus are identified as prophets, and prophecy was a recognized ministry in early Christianity.[7]

What is apocalyptic literature?

Apocalyptic literature is a genre in which divine foreknowledge of future events, especially of the end time, is revealed, usually to an individual, by a heavenly messenger or in a dream or vision; the word "apocalypse" means "revelation" or "unveiling." We find fully developed examples of apocalyptic literature in the Hebrew Bible in Daniel 7–12, in the Apocrypha in 2 Esdras, in the New Testament in the book of Revelation, and in many nonbiblical Jewish and Christian writings.

Apocalyptic literature is related to prophetic literature. Both feature direct divine revelation to an individual that often contains predictions about the future. Important examples in the prophets are Isaiah 24–27, Ezekiel 38–48, Joel 2:28–3:21, and Zechariah 9–14. These passages are also sources for Jesus's apocalyptic discourse in the Gospels (Matthew 24:4–36; Mark

13:5–37; Luke 21:8–36). Shorter apocalyptic elements occur throughout the prophets and the New Testament.

Over the ages, interpreters, especially Christian interpreters, have tried to see in the details, and especially the chronologies, of apocalyptic literature divine revelation about their own times and the immediate future. But none of the innumerable predictions of the end of the world have been correct, at least so far.

What are the principal genres in the New Testament?

The principal genres of the books of the New Testament are narrative histories: the Gospels and Acts of Apostles; letters, both to groups and to individuals; and apocalyptic literature in the book of Revelation. Because the New Testament books were written over less than a century, for the most part they are relatively unified and do not have complicated literary histories.

What is a gospel?

The English word "gospel" is an old translation of the Greek *euangelion*, "good news" or "good tidings," from which English words like "evangelist" are derived. In nonbiblical literature, an *euangelion* is a proclamation of some noteworthy positive event, such as a victory in battle or the accession of a ruler. An inscription from 9 BCE describes the Roman emperor Augustus's birthday as "the beginning of the good tidings for the world" and speaks of him as a savior and a god.[8]

In the New Testament, Mark's Gospel opens "The beginning of the good news of Jesus Christ, the son of God." The "gospel" proclaimed by Paul and other apostles is the good news about "Jesus Christ, raised from the dead" (2 Timothy 2:8).[9] Not surprisingly, then, the term "gospel" came to be used for the narratives about the life, preaching, death, and resurrection of Jesus. Scholars have long debated the precise genre of these narratives, but there is a growing consensus that they are modeled on ancient biographies whose primary purpose was to instruct by the example of their subject. They thus differ from modern biographies, which attempt to give a complete and accurate account of a person's life.

The four canonical Gospels, Matthew, Mark, Luke, and John, each have their own take on Jesus, which influenced which material each writer used and the order in which it is presented. Because they drew on different sources, and were written in different places for different audiences, they often disagree in detail. For example, the sign attached to Jesus's cross over his head reads as follows in the four Gospels:

This is Jesus, the king of the Jews. (Matthew 27:37)
The king of the Jews. (Mark 15:26)
This is the king of the Jews. (Luke 23:38)
Jesus of Nazareth, the king of the Jews. (John 19:19)

The differences here, and elsewhere, may be due to variations in oral or written sources, but in any case absolute accuracy does not seem to have been important.

In general, however, the first three Gospels are very close. They are called the "Synoptic Gospels" because when they are placed side by side, they look very similar.[10] Once Jesus's adult ministry begins, they have basically the same plot, and in recounting both his actions and his speeches they are often almost word for word the same. The fourth Gospel, however, is very different. Most of the material in it is not found in the other Gospels, and much of what it shares with them is presented differently, or in a different order. Most scholars think that Mark was probably written in the 70s, Matthew and Luke in the 80s, and John somewhat later. (See further pages 89–95.)

What is the genre of Acts of Apostles?

Acts of Apostles and the Gospel of Luke are a two-part work by the same author, as the prologue to Acts indicates (1:1; compare Luke 1:1–4). Acts can thus be understood as a kind of biography of the early Christian movement, focusing especially on the apostles Peter and Paul. The two parts were separated in order to keep the four Gospels together and not to disrupt the general chronological order of the canon. Acts uses many conventions of ancient historiography, especially attributing lengthy speeches to its principal characters. Like the Gospel of Luke, Acts was probably written in the 80s.[11] Although some of the events it recounts are referred to in Paul's letters, the author of Acts, writing at some remove from those events, presents a more irenic view of controversies that divided the earliest Christians, especially concerning observance of Jewish laws. At times in Acts, the writer switches from third-person narration to first-person-plural narration.[12] These "we" passages imply that the author, or a source that the author used, accompanied Paul on some of his travels and was an eyewitness to the events described in those passages. It is more likely, however, that this is a literary device, one found in other ancient historical works.

What are the "letters" in the New Testament?

Letters, in the sense of written communications, are a broad category. A letter can be personal correspondence; a more formal missive, often called an "epistle," sent to a group of persons; or an expository essay in the form of a letter. The structure of letters is relatively stable, from antiquity to the present. First comes the sender's identification, then the names of the addressee(s) and greetings to them. The body of the letter follows, and at the letter's end the sender will often send further greetings before signing. Many books of the Hebrew Bible and the Apocrypha contain letters in the course of their narratives, as, in the New Testament, do Acts of Apostles and Revelation.

The book known as the Letter of Jeremiah in the Apocrypha uses the same genre.

Several books of the New Testament belong to the category of personal correspondence. The best examples are Paul's letter to Philemon, and 3 John, from an anonymous "elder" to Gaius. The two letters to Timothy and the letter to Titus, known as "the Pastoral Epistles," are cast as letters from Paul to close associates in his ministry, but most scholars think that they are instructions for early Christian groups about church organization, personal conduct, and doctrine, by writers who used Paul's name as a pseudonym.

The other letters with names attached to them, whether authentically or not, are addressed to groups. Those in which Paul is the actual or the pseudonymous sender identify the addressees as Christian communities (or "churches") in cities or regions in the Roman Empire; this is also the case with 1 Peter. First and 2 John, 2 Peter, and the letters attributed to James and Jude identify the addressees more vaguely, for example as "those who have received faith" (2 Peter 1:1) and "those who are called" (Jude 1). These epistles were probably meant to be read aloud at the churches' liturgical gatherings.[13]

The contents of these epistles vary, but most, like the Pastoral Epistles, deal with issues of faith and morals, and sometimes report the sender's activities. They also occasionally give us details about how they were produced. At the end of Paul's letter to the Romans, the scribe or secretary who wrote the letter at Paul's dictation identifies himself: "I, Tertius, who wrote down this letter, greet you in the Lord" (Romans 16.22, New International Version). Furthermore, several times Paul himself pens a short note, a kind of postscript, as at the end of 1 Corinthians: "I, Paul, write this greeting with my own hand" (1 Corinthians 16:21, New Revised Standard Version).[14]

The book known as the letter to the Hebrews is not really a letter at all. Nowhere are either the sender or the recipient(s) precisely identified, and only at the very end are there greetings. It is, rather, a "word of exhortation" (13:22), perhaps a sermon turned into an essay. The title, which is not part of the original work, is derived from the main theme of the letter, the superiority of Christian belief and practice to those of Judaism. It may have been written to Jewish Christians in Rome: The greeting at the end from "those from Italy" (13:24) may refer to the addressees' former compatriots, living somewhere abroad.

What is the book of Revelation?

The only complete apocalypse in the Bible, the book of Revelation (a partial translation of its Greek title, *Apocalypsis Ioannou*, "the Revelation of John") is a detailed account by a man named John about a series of visions he had about events preceding the end of the world and about the coming of a new age. Most scholars think that this John is not to be identified as either the apostle John, the son of Zebedee, or the author(s) of the Gospel of John and 1, 2, and 3 John.

The book describes itself as a "prophecy" (1.3). After a brief introduction describing an angelic command given John on the island of Patmos, in the Aegean Sea, the book begins with the first of a series of sevens: letters to seven churches in Asia Minor (2.1–3:22). Then John has a vision of a scroll with seven seals, which are opened in succession accompanied by more visions (4.1–8.1). Then he sees seven angels with seven trumpets, which are blown in succession causing cosmic upheaval and plagues (8:6–9:21; 11:15–19), interrupted by other visions. There follows another series of unrelated visions—of a woman, a dragon, and two beasts that are defeated—and an anticipation of the ultimate victory of God and "the Lamb" (chapters 12–14). The next-to-last set of visions is seven angels with seven bowls containing supernatural elements of divine wrath. The fall of Babylon is described, along with the defeat of Satan. The book concludes with a vision of "a new heaven and a new earth" (21.1), including a new Jerusalem, and the promise that all the preceding visions will soon be fulfilled (chapters 21–22).

The book of Revelation draws extensively on earlier biblical texts, especially the books of Ezekiel, Daniel, and Joel, as well as on nonbiblical apocalyptic literature. Scholars generally agree that the book of Revelation is a thinly veiled attack on the Roman Empire, just as Daniel 7–12 was an attack on Antiochus IV Epiphanes, whose persecutions in the early second century BCE led to the revolt of the Maccabees. The "great whore" of Revelation is named "Babylon the great" (17:1, 5), but she sits on seven hills (17:9), like Rome, and 666, the notorious number of the beast on which she sits (13:18; 17:3), is a cipher for the emperor Nero.

4

AUTHORS AND AUTHORSHIP

Who wrote the Bible?

The simple fact is that we don't know who wrote much of the Bible. Although the names of apparent authors are found in many biblical books and parts of books, scholars have concluded that not all of those individuals wrote the works attributed to them. Many other parts of the Bible have no internal indication of authorship, although names were attached to some of them after they had been written; generally such attributions are unlikely, or at least unprovable. In both the Bible and other literature from the ancient world, writers often attributed their works to famous individuals from the past, to give them more prestige and authority. Ancient notions of authorship and intellectual property were often very different from ours, and just because a book says it was written by someone does not mean that person actually wrote it.[1]

Why does it matter who wrote the books of the Bible?

For fundamentalists both ancient and modern, the assertion that Moses, David, Solomon, Paul, and others did not write what the Bible says they did attacks its accuracy and thus its ultimate authority. For example, until modern times Jews and Christians with few exceptions believed that Moses was the author of the first five books of the Bible, even though Deuteronomy concludes with an account of Moses's death and burial. But fundamentalists have said that of course Moses did write the account of his own death and burial—after all, he was a prophet, and God could have revealed it to him.

Such naïve literalism is at odds with much scholarly study of the Bible since the Enlightenment, as we will see. For now, it is sufficient to recall that the larger and even many smaller parts of the Bible have complicated literary histories. In order to grasp their meanings, we have to try to unravel those histories. There is a difference between the Roman historian Suetonius's account of the reign of the emperor Claudius, and the fictional twentieth-century autobiography *I, Claudius* by Robert Graves; to understand them both, we need to be aware of who wrote them and when they were written. Similarly, in reading the Bible and many other ancient writings, we are kind of literary detectives: trying to determine not just provenance and date, but genre, purpose, and ultimately meaning from clues in texts that were written long ago.

How did the belief that Moses was the author of the Torah originate?

Its basis may be in passages that describe Moses writing down what God dictated to him; for example, "Moses wrote down all the words of the LORD" (Exodus 24:4).[2] Sometimes, too, Moses is credited with actual authorship of parts of the Torah, as in Deuteronomy 31:30; 33:1. So, in the Torah itself, Moses is presented both as a scribe or secretary and as an author, and eventually he was identified as the author of the first five books of the Bible, "the book of the *torah* of Moses, which the LORD had given to Israel" (Nehemiah 8:1).

Throughout the Bible, we find references to the "*torah* of Moses" (usually translated "the law of Moses," although "the teaching of Moses" is a better translation), and also to "the book of the *torah* of Moses" and "the book of Moses."[3] In many cases this clearly refers to the first five books of the Bible, the Torah. So, we are told, Joshua built an altar to the LORD, "just as Moses the servant of the LORD had commanded the Israelites, as it is written in the book of the law of Moses, 'an altar of unhewn stones, on which no iron tool has been used'" (Joshua 8:31); the quotation loosely cites Deuteronomy 27:5, itself derived from Exodus 20:25.[4] In the New Testament, "the Law" is similarly ascribed to Moses, and both Jesus and his contemporaries are described as quoting from the first five books of the Bible, again attributing them to Moses.[5]

But no internal evidence suggests that Moses was the author of the first five books of the Bible, the last four of which narrate his life. That narrative is biographical, not autobiographical, and as has been observed since the Middle Ages, Deuteronomy concludes with an account of Moses's death and burial, which he could not have written. This, along with anachronisms, internal inconsistencies, and contradictions in the Torah, make it clear that, absent a supernatural explanation, Moses wrote little if any of it. We will discuss the authorship of the Torah further in Chapter 6.

Did David write the psalms and other poems attributed to him?

Certainly not most of them. David was king of Israel in the early tenth century BCE. In the Masoretic Text, 73 of the 150 psalms have David's name attached to them in an editorial note or superscription at the beginning, using a Hebrew phrase which means something like "of David." But it is unclear exactly how to interpret this: Does it mean "by David" (that is, written by him) or "concerning David" (that is, about him)? In the later books of the Hebrew Bible, in other Jewish writings, and in the New Testament, David is often identified as the author when a psalm is quoted;[6] that is apparently what ancient editors of the book of Psalms thought as well. David was "the sweet psalmist of Israel" (2 Samuel 23:1, King James Version), described in the books of Samuel

and elsewhere as both a poet and a musician.[7] That reputa-
tion led to his being credited for many psalms, most of which
he probably did not write. For example, the superscription
to Psalm 51, like those to a dozen or so other psalms attributed to David, connects its content with an event in his life
narrated elsewhere in the Bible: "A psalm of David, when
the prophet Nathan came to him, after he had gone in to
Bathsheba"; this summarizes 2 Samuel 11–12, which tells of
David's adultery with Bathsheba and Nathan's rebuke of
David's sin. Although the psalm is a prayer of repentance,
David did not write it, at least not in its present form, for
its last two verses refer to the destruction of Jerusalem (also
called Zion) in the sixth century BCE, long after David lived:

> Do good to Zion in your good pleasure;
>   rebuild the walls of Jerusalem,
> then you will delight in right sacrifices,
>   in burnt offerings and whole burnt offerings;
>   then bulls will be offered on your altar.

Other psalms attributed to David mention the Temple, which
David's son and successor Solomon built only after his father's
death; again, David could not have written them.

A few other poems are attributed to David elsewhere in the
Bible. In 2 Samuel, David is described as the performer, and
presumably the author and composer, of an elegy for Saul,
his predecessor as king, and Jonathan, Saul's son and David's
friend (1:17–27); a lament for Abner, Saul's cousin and general
(3:33–34); a hymn praising and thanking God (22:1–51, virtually identical to Psalm 18); and "the last words of David"
(23:1–7). David is likely the author of the first two of these, and
possibly also the last.

As time went on, more and more of the psalms were attributed to David. The Septuagint, the ancient Greek translation
of the Hebrew Bible, credits him with 84, the New Testament
with two not attributed to him in the Hebrew text,[8] and some

rabbinic traditions with all 150.[9] Some Christian canons include Psalm 151, recognized as "outside the number" but still considered scripture and attributed to David. A Psalms manuscript among the Dead Sea Scrolls claims that David wrote 3,600 psalms, in addition to another 450 songs for various rituals and holy days, illustrating the tendency to give David more and more credit for ancient Israelite hymnody.

Did Solomon write all the books attributed to him?

David's successor as king of Israel was his son Solomon, who is given credit for several biblical and apocryphal books, and parts of others. In 1 Kings, Solomon is described as a ruler to whom God had given greater wisdom than any of his contemporaries, and thus as one who wrote a great deal of what scholars call "wisdom literature":

> He composed three thousand proverbs, and his songs numbered a thousand and five. He would speak of trees, from the cedar that is in Lebanon to the hyssop that grows in the wall; he would speak of animals, and birds, and reptiles, and fish. (1 Kings 4:32–33; see also Sirach 47:14–17)

Given this probably legendary catalogue, it is unsurprising that three collections of proverbs in the book of Proverbs are credited to Solomon (see Proverbs 1:1; 10:1; 25:1). But we have no way of determining which of the proverbs, if any, Solomon himself actually wrote.

Two psalms are attributed to Solomon as well. Psalm 72 is a prayer for the king and a "king's son." It asks that "gold of Sheba be given to him" (verse 15), reminiscent of the 120 talents (several tons!) of gold that the queen of Sheba brought to Solomon,[10] and it mentions Tarshish, another place associated with Solomon.[11] Psalm 127 is also attributed to Solomon, no doubt because of words in its opening verses:

> Unless the LORD builds the house,
> those who build it labor in vain. . . .
> for he gives sleep to his beloved.

This calls to mind Solomon's building the "house of the LORD," the first Temple in Jerusalem, and his birth name, Jedidiah (2 Samuel 12:25), which means "beloved of Yahweh."

The author of the book of Qoheleth (more familiarly known as Ecclesiastes) apparently identifies himself near the beginning of the book named for him: "I, Qoheleth, was king over Israel in Jerusalem" (1:12, New American Bible, Revised Edition), and an editor further identifies him as David's son (1:1) and as wise (12:9). This would make Qoheleth Solomon himself. But Solomon cannot have been the author, because the text uses words of Persian origin that would not have been known to Solomon or anyone else in Israel in the tenth century BCE when he lived. Those words, and other features of the book's language, make it clear that it was written in the fifth or fourth century BCE, which means that a now-anonymous author adopted the pseudonym Solomon, using the epithet Qoheleth, which means "the gatherer," perhaps the one who gathered wisdom (see 1:16).

Solomon is also given credit for writing the Song of Solomon, which is an anthology of often-erotic love poems.[12] This attribution is probably responsible for the book's inclusion in the canon, but Solomon did not write it. To be sure, he is mentioned half a dozen times in the text, but by speakers other than himself. Behind the attribution of the Song to Solomon is likely the memory of his enormous harem—seven hundred princesses and three hundred secondary wives.[13]

The Wisdom of Solomon, one of the Apocrypha, is a work composed in Greek in the late first century BCE or the early first century CE. Its anonymous author adopts the persona of Solomon, recalling God's mission for him:

> You have chosen me to be king of your people
> and to be judge over your sons and daughters.
> You have given command to build a temple on
>   your holy mountain,
> and an altar in the city of your habitation,
> a copy of the holy tent that you prepared from the
>   beginning. (Wisdom 9:7–8)

He prays for wisdom (see 1 Kings 3:9), so that he may be worthy of the throne of his father (Wisdom 9:10–12). Postbiblical books with Solomon as the author's pseudonym include the Psalms of Solomon and the Odes of Solomon.

Did the prophets write the books named after them?

Not in their entirety. All of the prophetic books were shaped by anonymous editors; the books' openings, or superscriptions, were written about the prophets, not by them. Here is the beginning of the superscription to the book of Jeremiah, the longest superscription of any of the prophetic books:

> The words of Jeremiah son of Hilkiah, of the priests who were in Anathoth in the land of Benjamin, to whom the word of the LORD came in the days of King Josiah son of Amon of Judah, in the thirteenth year of his reign. (Jeremiah 1:1–2, New Revised Standard Version [NRSV])

This is immediately followed by a report in the first person of Jeremiah's call: "Now the word of the LORD came to me" (1:4). Throughout the book of Jeremiah, as in several other prophetic books, we find alternation between such biographical and autobiographical materials; the former, at least, are clearly not from the prophets themselves.

Such combinations of material indicate that many of the prophetic books have a literary history, in some cases quite long. Because the words of the prophets were believed to have enduring significance, they were often updated for new audiences in new circumstances. Moreover, in some cases, most notably Isaiah, there developed something like schools of the prophets, like the philosophical schools of ancient Greece, which continued writing texts using the same vocabulary as the original prophet and developing that prophet's ideas. So, just as Socrates did not say everything that the later dialogues of Plato and his successors put in his mouth, so too parts of the book of Isaiah were written not by the prophet Isaiah himself, who lived in the late eighth and early seventh centuries BCE, but by members of his school as much as two centuries later.[14]

Who wrote the books of the Apocrypha?

Only one book of the Apocrypha has a known author, Sirach, a scribe in Jerusalem in the early second century BCE. The translation of the book into Greek was made by Sirach's grandson, who tells us in his prologue about his grandfather and also that he made the translation in Egypt.

The unnamed author of 2 Maccabees tells us that his work is an abridgement of a five-volume work that no longer survives by Jason of Cyrene, a city in Libya, who is otherwise unknown. All other books of the Apocrypha with presumed authors' names attached to them are pseudonymous.

Who wrote the books of the New Testament?

In some of the books of the New Testament, the author identifies himself by name. These are the letters of Paul, James, Peter, and Jude, along with the book of Revelation, which names its author as John.

Nearly all scholars agree that Paul himself wrote several of the letters attributed to him; these are Romans, 1 and 2 Corinthians, Galatians, Philippians, 1 Thessalonians, and Philemon. Another seven letters identify their author as Paul, but a majority of modern scholars think that most if not all of these are pseudonymous. They may have been written by disciples of Paul, but it is unlikely that Paul himself wrote most of them, because their vocabulary and theology are different from those of the genuine letters. Although the letter to the Hebrews does not name its author, it has often been attributed to Paul, in part because of the reference to his companion and associate Timothy in the conclusion.[15] But because its language and content are so different from the genuine letters of Paul, many ancient and most modern scholars have doubted that he wrote it.[16]

The same is true of the letters attributed to other apostles. Most scholars think it unlikely that the author of 1 and 2 Peter was the apostle himself, or that Jude wrote the letter that has his name. The author of the letter of James is probably meant to be identified as James, Jesus's brother[17] and also one of Jesus's "twelve apostles," a group of Jesus's closest followers, although it is unlikely that he wrote it.[18]

The Gospels are a special case. Nowhere in the actual text of any Gospel do authors identify themselves. The names traditionally given to the authors of the four Gospels are found elsewhere in the New Testament and were attached to the Gospels by the late second century to give them greater authority. The best known are Matthew and John, both of whom were among the twelve apostles. Mark is probably the individual known as John Mark, and sometimes simply as either John or Mark, who was an associate of both Peter and Paul (Acts 12:12, 25; 15:37; Philemon 24). The author of both the Gospel of Luke and Acts of Apostles is identified as Luke, another associate of Paul, called "the beloved physician" (Colossians 4:14; see also Philemon 24).

The author of the Gospel of John calls himself "the disciple whom Jesus loved" (21:20, 24; see also 13:23), who since the second century has been identified as the apostle John, the son of Zebedee (Mark 3:17). In addition to the Gospel of John, three letters (1, 2, and 3 John) also are credited to this apostle John. But 1 John is anonymous, and in 2 and 3 John, the author calls himself simply "the elder." Still, because all four books use much of the same thematic vocabulary, many ancient and some modern scholars have thought that a single author wrote them all. More likely, however, different members of what has been called a "Johannine community" separately produced these four books.

The book of Revelation opens: "The revelation of Jesus Christ, which God gave him . . . by sending his angel to his servant John, who testified to the word of God and to the testimony of Jesus Christ, even to all that he saw" (1:1–2). Although this is reminiscent of the conclusion of the Gospel of John (21:24), toward the end of Revelation the author speaks of the "twelve apostles" as though he were not one of them (21:14). So, most scholars think that the two books had different authors, and that the author of Revelation was not the apostle John but someone else with the same name.[19]

Like their Jewish predecessors and contemporaries, Christian writers also produced many pseudepigrapha that did not become canonical. Examples include the Gospels of Thomas, Philip, Peter, and James; Acts of Andrew, John, and Paul; and additional letters attributed to Paul. Many of these were early recognized as not from the apostles themselves, and some were from groups that were viewed as heretical by mainstream religious authorities, so they did not become canonical.

When was the Bible written?

The parts of the Bible that are probably the oldest are a few poems (or parts of them) in the Hebrew Bible, such as the Blessing of Jacob (Genesis 49), the Song of the Sea (Exodus 15), the oracles of Balaam (Numbers 23–24), the Song of Deborah

(Judges 5), and David's lament over Saul and Jonathan (2 Samuel 1:19–27). Of these, the oldest may be the Song of Deborah, dating perhaps to the twelfth or eleventh century BCE, and the rest may be a century or two later. The basis for this early dating, accepted by many but not all scholars, is both the archaic language of the poems and their content. The latest book of the Hebrew Bible is the book of Daniel, parts of which date to the early second century BCE, based on internal historical allusions. Most of the Apocrypha were written in the Hellenistic and early Roman periods, from the third century BCE to the first century CE. The books of the New Testament were written over a relatively brief period, from the mid-first to the early second centuries CE.

But many of the books of the Hebrew Bible, especially the longer ones, were not written by one author as a single unified work. Rather, in their present form, they are the end product of a process that often extended over several centuries. Scholars have devoted countless tomes to trying to unravel the underlying stages of the formation of the books and their dates.

Here is one example. The last book of the Torah, Deuteronomy, is at first glance the text of Moses's farewell address to the Israelites before his death, which probably occurred in the thirteenth century BCE. It begins: "These are the words that Moses addressed to all Israel on the other side of the Jordan" (1:1, New Jewish Publication Society Translation [NJPS]). Moses died on Mount Nebo, which is east of the Jordan River; the introduction to his address, then, was written by someone west of the Jordan, for whom Mount Nebo would have been "on the other side," and not by Moses himself.

As we read on in Deuteronomy, we discover that it is not a single speech, but several, each with its own introduction:

On the other side of the Jordan, in the land of Moab, Moses began to interpret this teaching,[20] saying . . . (1:5, my translation)

> This is the Teaching that Moses set before the
> Israelites . . . beyond the Jordan. . . . Moses summoned all
> Israel, and said to them . . . (4:44–5:1, NJPS)

> These are the words of the covenant that the LORD com-
> manded Moses to make with the Israelites in the land
> of Moab. . . . Moses summoned all Israel, and said to
> them . . . (29:1–2, NRSV)

At the end of Deuteronomy, we find further words attributed to Moses, in two poems. The first, known as "the Song
of Moses," is introduced as follows: "Then Moses recited
the words of this song" (31:30, NRSV), and the second,
"the Blessing of Moses," is introduced: "This is the blessing
with which Moses, the man of God, blessed the Israelites
before his death. He said . . ." (33:1, NRSV). Probably neither of these poems was written by Moses, but their inclusion in the final form of the book further complicates our
understanding of it.

In various parts of the book, we find some clues to dating.
In the early sixth century BCE, the Babylonians, from distant
Mesopotamia, invaded Judah and deported several thousand of its inhabitants to Babylonia; others fled to Egypt.[21] In
Deuteronomy, we find references to these events at the beginning and the end of the book. Toward the end of Moses's
first speech, he warns the Israelites that if they worship idols,
"The LORD will scatter you among the peoples. . . . There you
will serve other gods made by human hands, objects of wood
and stone" (4:27–28, NRSV). And in the conclusion of Moses's
second speech, the lengthy series of divine punishments that
will be inflicted on the Israelites if they fail to observe God's
commandments and laws includes these:

> The LORD will bring a nation from far away, from the
> end of the earth, to swoop down on you like an eagle, a
> nation whose language you do not understand. . . . The

LORD will scatter you among all peoples, from one end
of the earth to the other; and there you shall serve other
gods, of wood and stone, which neither you nor your ancestors have known. . . . The LORD will bring you back in
ships to Egypt. (Deuteronomy 28:49, 64, 68, NRSV)

The punishments proclaimed in Deuteronomy thus are prophecy after the fact, reflecting the history of Judah in the early
sixth century, and those sections of Deuteronomy should be
dated no earlier than that.

In 538 BCE, the Persian king Cyrus, having defeated the
Babylonians, allowed Judean exiles in Babylonia to return to
Judah. Moses's third speech refers to this:

When all these things have happened to you . . . then the
LORD your God will restore your fortunes and have com-
passion on you, gathering you again from all the peoples
among which the LORD your God has scattered you. . . .
The LORD your God will bring you into the land that
your ancestors possessed. (Deuteronomy 30:1–5, NRSV)

Parts of Deuteronomy thus date no earlier than the late sixth
century.

But does the entire book? In the late seventh century BCE, the
Judean king Josiah undertook a sweeping religious reform, inspired, we are told, by the discovery of a "book" in the Temple.[22]
The details of the reform correspond closely to commandments in Deuteronomy, pushing back parts of Deuteronomy to
at least the seventh century. As its English name, which means
"second law," suggests, Deuteronomy draws on and revises
earlier legal traditions. Thus, underlying it is even older material. So we should think of a "Deuteronomic school," active
for two or more centuries, which revised and expanded its
core text to suit changing circumstances. As it turns out, this

school was also responsible for editing the Former Prophets, the books of Joshua, Judges, Samuel, and Kings.

All of the other books of the Pentateuch, all of the Former Prophets, and many of the Latter Prophets and the Writings have similar literary histories. In dating these books, we need to consider not just when they reached their final form, but the stages that preceded their final form. That is why the answers to the questions when and by whom the Bible was written are often very complicated.

5

THE CONTEXTS OF THE BIBLE

*Why is it important to study the contexts in which
the biblical writers lived?*

Because the Bible was not written in a vacuum, but in a world—
or rather, many worlds—that are different from ours, understanding those worlds helps us understand the Bible. Reading
the Bible is like reading the libretto of an opera or the text of a
play. Studying the geography, history, and material culture of
the biblical writers gets us closer to the worlds in which they
lived—like seeing the opera or play performed with scenery,
costumes, props, and even sounds. In this chapter, we will
survey several aspects of those worlds, and we will also take
a look at how archaeology sheds light on the Bible.

What is the Fertile Crescent?

The Fertile Crescent is a relatively narrow band of arable land
stretching northward from the Nile River valley in Egypt along
the Mediterranean coast to northwestern Syria, then eastward
to the valleys of the Euphrates and Tigris rivers and south to
the Persian Gulf. Beneath the arc of the crescent is a vast desert
that extends southward into the Arabian peninsula. Beginning
about 4000 BCE, complex urban societies developed at the two
ends of this crescent, in the Nile Valley and in Mesopotamia—a

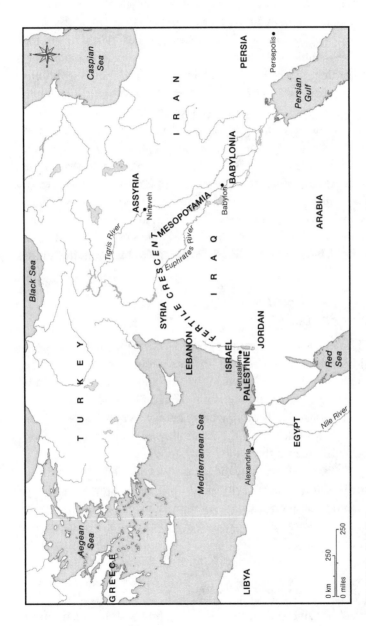

Map 5.1 The Near East

Greek term for the region between the Euphrates and the Tigris, now mostly in modern Iraq.

The Fertile Crescent is the locale for most narratives in the Hebrew Bible, the Apocrypha, and the Gospels. For example, according to Genesis, Abraham's father, Terah, moved his family from southern Mesopotamia to northern Syria; then Abraham moved to Canaan—modern Israel and Palestine—and for a time lived in Egypt. Abraham's grandson Jacob moved his family from Canaan to Egypt, and then, according to the book of Exodus, several generations later Moses led the Israelites out of Egypt to the border of Canaan. Over and over, these migrations—some voluntary, some forced—repeated, as with the exile of Judeans to Babylonia in southern Mesopotamia in the sixth century BCE, and the account of Mary, Joseph, and Jesus fleeing to Egypt and then moving to Nazareth in Galilee in northern Canaan.[1]

What is the Levant?

The Levant is a term that scholars often use for the western side of the Fertile Crescent, the lands immediately east of the Mediterranean Sea between Turkey and Egypt, today comprising western Syria, Lebanon, Israel, Palestine, and Jordan. It is thus a subdivision of what is known as both the Near East and the Middle East. Like those phrases, it has a Eurocentric perspective, meaning "the rising" (of the sun).

For much of antiquity the Levant was divided into relatively small entities, mostly city-states and small kingdoms. They shared a common culture, worshipped many of the same gods and goddesses, and spoke and eventually wrote in closely related languages.

What is the topography of Israel?

Israel has five principal zones that run south to north. From west to east, these are:

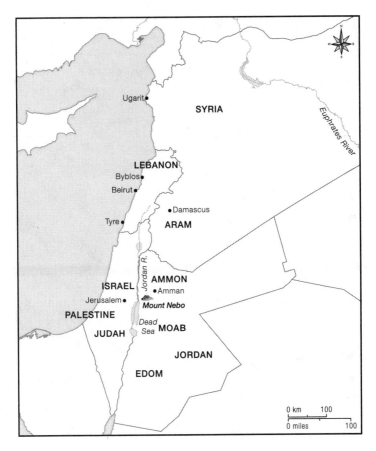

Map 5.2 The Levant

- The coastal plain. In antiquity, this was often swampy, and there were few natural harbors.
- The foothills or Shephelah. A principal route from Egypt to the north, used by travelers, traders, and armies, lay between the coastal plain and the foothills.
- The hill country. Elevations increase from south to north; Jerusalem is about 2,500 feet above sea level, northern Galilee about 3,500 feet above sea level, and Mount Hermon in the far north is over 9,000 feet above sea level.

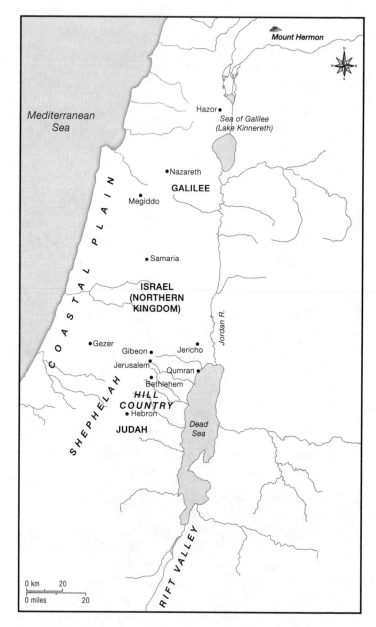

Map 5.3 Ancient Israel

- The Rift Valley. Immediately east of the hill country is part of a large geological fault line that extends from northern Lebanon south to the northeastern arm of the Red Sea. Much of it is below sea level; for example, the Sea of Galilee (also known as Lake Kinnereth) is about 700 feet below sea level, and the Dead Sea, into which the Jordan River flows, is about 1,400 feet below sea level, the lowest elevation on the earth's land mass.[2]
- The Transjordanian plateau. Immediately east of the Rift Valley, the land rapidly rises, with elevations again several thousand feet above sea level.

Thus, although the distance from Jerusalem to Amman is only forty-five miles as the crow flies, in that short distance the elevations change from about 2,500 feet above sea level in Jerusalem to almost 1,000 feet below sea level at the Jordan River crossing, to about 3,500 ft above sea level in Amman. Thus, from almost every direction, in the Bible one goes up to Jerusalem and down from it.[3]

How does historical geography help us understand the Bible?

Historical geography is the study of how the geography of the past relates to that of the present. One way this works is in the identification of ancient places. Sometimes, like Jerusalem, Tyre, Athens, and Rome, these places have been more or less continuously inhabited for many centuries, and their names have remained the same. Sometimes the name of a site in ruins is preserved in local oral tradition, or in the name of a later village or town nearby; for example, the site near the village of el-Jib north of Jerusalem was frequently identified as biblical Gibeon, an identification confirmed by the discovery there of wine jars inscribed with the name of the city.

Historical geography begins in the Bible itself, when alternate names are given for locations such as Jerusalem and Hebron.[4]

From late antiquity onward, scholars and pilgrims have continued to identify biblical toponyms with contemporary sites, although the location of many sites is still unknown or disputed.

Are all the places mentioned in the Bible real places?

Some are not. For example, the Garden of Eden is not real but mythical, "the garden of God" planted by the LORD himself.[5] Although from it flowed four rivers, Pishon, Gihon, the Tigris, and the Euphrates, this does not correspond to actual geography: The Tigris and the Euphrates are in Mesopotamia, but Gihon (meaning "gusher") is the name of a spring in Jerusalem some five hundred miles west of Mesopotamia, and Pishon is unknown. This lush garden contained all ornamental and all fruit trees, as well as the tree of life, whose fruit makes one immortal, and the mysterious "tree of the knowledge of good and evil" whose fruit was forbidden. Also in the garden were all species of birds and of animals, which the LORD God had created as potential partners for the first man, later to be called Adam; and a talking snake, later to be called Satan, who enticed Eve to eat the forbidden fruit. Similarly belonging more to myth than to history are other places mentioned early in the Bible, such as the Tower of Babel and Sodom and Gomorrah.

What is the history of the ancient Near East?

Writ large, the history of the ancient Near East is a history of competing and successive empires. For most of the biblical period—from about the fifteenth century BCE to the second century CE—the Levant was under the control of its more powerful neighbors—Egypt to its south-southwest; the Hittites in Asia Minor (roughly modern Turkey); then Assyria and Babylonia to the northeast in Mesopotamia; Persia, east of Mesopotamia; and eventually Greece, and then Rome, to the west.

During most of the second millennium BCE, Egypt controlled the southern Levant. This is the period covered by the biblical writers in Genesis 12–50 and the books of Exodus through Joshua. But in the late second millennium and the early first millennium BCE, Egypt had lost control of the southern Levant because of foreign invaders and internal struggles. During this period smaller kingdoms emerged, including Edom, Moab and Ammon east of the Rift Valley, Israel to its west, and Tyre and Aram-Damascus to Israel's north and northeast, respectively. Initially, as the book of Judges relates, Israel was a loose confederation of tribes (traditionally twelve), which according to the books of Samuel developed into a monarchy ruled first by Saul, and then by David and by his son Solomon. We have no nonbiblical confirmation of these events and persons, and scholars disagree about the extent of their kingdom and even about their status: Were they really kings, or just local chieftains?

After the death of Solomon about 928 BCE, what had apparently been a "united monarchy" split into two kingdoms: Judah in the south, where David's descendants would continue to rule in Jerusalem, its capital city, for some three and a half centuries, and Israel in the north, ruled by a succession of dynasties, eventually from its capital in Samaria, until 722 BCE. The history of these two kingdoms—sometimes allies, sometimes rivals—is found in the books of Kings and Chronicles, as well as in many of the Latter Prophets. We also know something of this history from nonbiblical sources. In fact, the more frequently characters, events, and places known from the Bible are mentioned in nonbiblical sources, the more ominous is the situation of those living in the southern Levant, as foreign powers took greater and greater control of the region.

TIMELINE*

Dates	Dominant Powers in the Levant	Events	Persons
ca. 1550–1200 BCE	**Egypt (south), Hittites (north)**		
ca. 1250 BCE		Exodus from Egypt	Moses
ca. 1210		Entry of Israelites into land of Canaan	Joshua
ca. 1200–1050	**No dominant powers**		
ca. 1150–1050		Period of the judges and rise of the Philistines	
ca. 1020	—	Establishment of the Israelite monarchy	Saul
ca. 1000–965	—	United Monarchy	David
ca. 968–928	—		Solomon
ca. 945–525	**Egypt (south)**		
ca. 928		Split between the northern kingdom of Israel and the southern kingdom of Judah	
ca. 900–609	**Assyria**		
722		Assyrian conquest of northern kingdom of Israel	
701		Assyrian siege of Jerusalem	Isaiah; Hezekiah
609–539	**Babylonia**		
609		Babylonian defeat of Assyria	
597		Babylonian siege of Jerusalem	Jehoiachin; Jeremiah; Ezekiel
586		Babylonian destruction of Jerusalem	Zedekiah; Jeremiah; Ezekiel

539–332	**Persia**	
539	Persian capture of Babylon	Cyrus the Great
538	Cyrus allows Judean exiles to return	
520–515	Rebuilding of Jerusalem Temple	
ca. 450	Missions of Ezra and Nehemiah	
332–63	**Greece**	
330	Alexander the Great defeats Persians	
167–164	Revolt of the Maccabees	
63 BCE–330 CE	**Rome**	
ca. 30 CE	Crucifixion of Jesus of Nazareth	
ca. 50–60	Letters of Paul	
66–73	First Jewish Revolt against Rome	
70	Romans capture Jerusalem and destroy the Temple	
ca. 70–80	Gospel of Mark	
ca. 80–90	Gospels of Matthew and Luke	
ca. 90–100	Gospel of John	
ca. 132–35	Second Jewish Revolt against Rome	

*Earlier dates are approximate, and some dates are disputed.

From about 900 to the late seventh century BCE, Assyria in northern Mesopotamia became the dominant power in the Near East, first conquering its southern rival Babylonia and then rapidly extending its control into the Levant and eventually even into Egypt. The Assyrians incorporated Tyre, Aram-Damascus, Ammon, Moab, and Edom into their empire as vassals, and in 722 eliminated the northern kingdom of Israel because its king had refused to pay the required levy. When Hezekiah, the king of Judah, similarly refused in the late eighth century, the Assyrians laid siege to Jerusalem and compelled him to pay enormous tribute.

Although the Assyrians captured northern Egypt in the early seventh century, by the end of that century the Assyrian Empire was overextended, and eventually fell to the Babylonians in 609. The Babylonians took over the Assyrian Empire, and quickly quashed rebellions by Jehoiakim and Zedekiah, kings of Judah. They first besieged Jerusalem in 597, exiling to Babylonia Jehoiakim's successor, Jehoiachin, and several thousand of Judah's elite, including the priest and prophet Ezekiel. Then, in response to another rebellion by Jehoiachin's uncle Zedekiah, the Babylonians returned, besieged Jerusalem again, and destroyed it in 586, exiling several hundred more to Babylonia.

Babylonian control of the Near East came to an end in 539 BCE, when King Cyrus II (the Great) of Persia captured Babylon. For the next two centuries, the Levant, and northern Egypt and Asia Minor as well, were largely under Persian control. In the fourth century, however, Greeks under the leadership of Philip II of Macedon moved eastward into Asia Minor, and Alexander the Great, Philip's son, took over Egypt in 332 and captured the Persian capital of Persepolis a year later.

Alexander's rule inaugurated what is known as the Hellenistic period, when Greek language and culture became a kind of veneer on the preexisting cultures of the Near East. Alexander's successors divided up his empire, and political entities in the Levant enjoyed a quasi-independence most of the time. But by the early first century BCE, Greek rule of the Levant was replaced by that of the Romans, who divided the Levant into various provinces and turned the Mediterranean into what has been called a "Roman lake." The Roman Empire was brutal in its suppression of rebellion, as exemplified by the capture and destruction of Jerusalem in response to the First and Second Jewish Revolts in 70 CE and 135 CE.

Which major biblical characters are mentioned in contemporaneous nonbiblical sources?

Leaving aside foreign rulers and the like, most of whom are known from nonbiblical sources, not that many characters in the Hebrew Bible are mentioned elsewhere. About a dozen are kings of Israel and Judah, mentioned in Assyrian and Babylonian texts mostly as paying tribute to Assyrian and Babylonian rulers. Omri, king of Israel in the ninth century BCE, is also mentioned in one of the few Moabite texts, and Sanballat, governor of Samaria in fifth century BCE, is mentioned in a papyrus from Elephantine in southern Egypt. None of the Jewish characters in the Apocrypha are mentioned in contemporaneous nonbiblical texts, not even Judas Maccabeus and his brothers. For the New Testament, Pontius Pilate, the governor of Judea (as Judah was now called) who oversaw the execution of Jesus, and Gallo, the Roman proconsul of Corinth mentioned in Acts 18:12, are both attested in contemporaneous inscriptions as well as in nonbiblical sources. The late first-century CE historian Josephus mentions in his writings King Herod and three of his children; Annas and Caiaphas, two first-century CE high priests;[6] John the Baptist; Jesus; and James, the brother of Jesus. Although Josephus's references are not exactly contemporaneous, they are nearly so, as are scattered references to Jesus in early second-century Roman writers.

Largely because both ancient Israel and the earliest Christian communities were relatively insignificant, so far at least we have no nonbiblical contemporaneous mentions of David and Solomon, of any of the prophets, or of Peter or Paul.[7] Moving further back in time, none of the characters in the Pentateuch are found in contemporaneous nonbiblical sources; from the perspective of the Egyptian rulers of the Levant, they were apparently unimportant—extras, as it were, on the stage of world history. Not even the Exodus from Egypt and its associated plagues and the drowning of the Egyptian army are mentioned in any contemporaneous sources. However, a victory stela of the Egyptian pharaoh Merneptah dated to 1209 BCE lists Israel among other defeated enemies of Egypt; this is the earliest mention of Israel in a nonbiblical source.[8]

How were the writers of the Hebrew Bible influenced by texts from other cultures?

Because of the common culture of the Levant, we find parallels between most genres of the Hebrew Bible and those of other literatures. Sometimes direct borrowing probably occurred, and sometimes shared literary and mythological traditions explain the parallels. Here we will focus on examples of close parallels.

Ancient Near Eastern cultures whose literature has survived or been discovered all have creation myths. Like those in Genesis 1 and 2, they can describe creation by a divinely spoken word or the creation of humans from clay. Mesopotamian myths also feature stories of a great flood, one of which, in the *Gilgamesh* epic, has close parallels to the story of Noah in Genesis 6–9. In both, the hero is divinely instructed to build a boat to escape the imminent flood, and to bring on board family and animals. After the storm abates, the boat comes to rest on a mountain, and the hero releases birds to see if it is safe to disembark; when the last bird released does not return, the hero knows he can leave the boat. Then he offers a sacrifice, whose odor pleases the gods or, in the case of Noah, the LORD. The closeness of the parallels is likely the result of direct borrowing. This also suggests that Noah's ark should be searched for in texts rather than on the ground.

From Egypt, we have collections of love poems teeming with natural imagery in which the lovers call each other "brother" and "sister" and vividly describe each other's bodies, all features of the Song of Solomon. Of the many collections of proverbs in ancient Egyptian literature, one, the *Instruction of Amenenope*, which dates to the late second millennium BCE, has thirty sections; in the biblical book of Proverbs, one part ("The words of the wise," 22:17–24:22) describes its contents as "thirty sayings of admonition and knowledge" (22:20), and many of the proverbs in it closely resemble those in the Egyptian text. It seems likely, then, that this *Instruction* was known in scribal schools in ancient Israel and was one source that the compliers of the biblical book used. Finally, several verses in Psalm 104 are close to lines in the fourteenth-century BCE Egyptian hymn to the Aten, the deified solar disk.

At the site of the ancient city of Ugarit, on the Mediterranean coast in northern Syria, archaeologists have discovered about two thousand texts written in Ugaritic, a language closely related to Hebrew. Among them are several incomplete myths and epics dating to the late second millennium BCE in their present form. Many aspects of these texts have similarities to biblical texts. One similarity concerns poetry: Both biblical and Ugaritic poetry have as their main formal feature a device known as "parallelism." In this device, a single thought is expressed in two or three lines by the use of repetition, synonyms, antonyms, or extensions. Here is an example from the myth of the Ugaritic storm god Baal, who is being addressed by one of the gods:

> Let me tell you, Prince Baal,
> > let me repeat, Rider on the Clouds:
> Now, your enemy, Baal,
> > now you will kill your enemy,
> > now you will annihilate your foe.

You will take your eternal kingship,
    your dominion forever and ever.[9]

Both the parallelism and the content are familiar from biblical poetry:

Behold, your enemies, O Lord,
    behold, your enemies have perished,
        all evildoers have been scattered. (Psalm 92:9, my
    translation)
Your kingdom is an eternal kingdom,
    your rule is for all generations. (Psalm 145:13, my
    translation)

Moreover, like Baal, the Israelite deity is often described as a storm god, and he is also called by the epithet "rider on the clouds" (Psalm 68:4). These parallels are examples of shared culture rather than direct borrowing, because Ugarit was destroyed before Israel had fully developed.

In the book of Numbers, the king of Moab hires the prophet Balaam to curse the Israelites, who are passing through Moab. The oracles that Balaam delivers, under divine inspiration, instead bless Israel. Some of the language in those oracles is also found in a text written on plaster discovered at Tell Deir Alla in the eastern Jordan Valley. In that text, dating to about 800 BCE and written in a local dialect, the seer Balaam reports a vision he had received. The authors of Numbers have apparently made a Transjordanian prophet the bearer of an anti-Transjordanian revelation.

How were the writers of the Apocrypha influenced by texts from other cultures?

Because most of the Apocrypha were written in the Hellenistic period, they exhibit significant Greek influence. A prominent example is Wisdom of Solomon, written in elegant Greek probably in Alexandria, Egypt, in late biblical times. Its author urges his Jewish audience to live righteous lives, and retells some Pentateuchal narratives, especially the Exodus from Egypt. But this recapitulation of the biblical story is infused with vocabulary and concepts derived from Greek philosophy. Thus, like some Greek thinkers, the author calls the world the "cosmos" and the underworld "Hades," believes that the soul of a righteous person existed before birth and will survive after death, and praises the four cardinal virtues of self-control, prudence, justice, and courage known from Plato and other Greek writers.

Other books of the Apocrypha use many genres known from Greek literature. The style of 1 and 2 Maccabees owes as much to that of Greek historians as to biblical precedents. Third Maccabees, originally written in Greek, also probably in Alexandria, shares the style of many Greek novellas, and 4 Maccabees includes a kind of philosophic dialogue. Although Sirach lived in Jerusalem, he had traveled widely[10] and seems to have been familiar with Greek literature; his comparison of human generations to leaves on a tree is very close to a famous simile in the *Iliad*.[11]

How were the writers of the New Testament influenced by texts from other cultures?

Because the New Testament writers, most of whom themselves were Jewish, accepted the Jewish scriptures as authoritative, quotations from and allusions to those scriptures recur repeatedly in the New Testament. For the New Testament writers, the Jewish scriptures were also revelations of a divine plan fulfilled in Jesus's life and death. Matthew interprets more than a dozen quotations from the Jewish scriptures in this way, and Luke has Jesus say: "Everything written about me in the law of Moses, the prophets, and the psalms must be fulfilled" (24:44, New Revised Standard Version). In his letter to the Romans,

Paul quotes the Jewish scriptures dozens of times, and the book of Revelation has many allusions to the books of Ezekiel and Daniel, among others.

The Jewish scriptures were also a source of plot elements in the narratives of the Gospels and Acts of Apostles. The birth and infancy narratives about Jesus in Matthew and Luke draw from those about Isaac, Moses, Samson, and Samuel. Similarly, Jesus multiplied food, raised the dead, and was taken up to heaven, just as is reported of the prophet Elijah. Finally, many of the details of Jesus's suffering and death in all of the Gospels are based on the Jewish scriptures, "which say it must happen in this way" (Matthew 26:54).

But the New Testament writers were also writing in Greek, in the Hellenized Roman Empire. In Acts of Apostles, for example, we find elements of narrative history and historical fiction such as travelogues, shipwrecks, and escapes from prison, along with dialogues and speeches attributed to principal characters; these genres and many more are known not only from the Jewish scriptures but also from many Greco-Roman works. In the letters and epistles, we also find frequent use of Greek rhetorical devices, as well as the household codes also known from Greco-Roman literature. So, to interpret the New Testament writings, we need to take into account not only their scriptural antecedents but also how their language and literary themes were used in nonbiblical writings, just as we should with the Hebrew Bible and its ancient Near Eastern parallels.

How does archaeology enhance our understanding of the Bible?

Archaeology provides huge quantities of data, much of which is relevant for biblical interpretation. Over the last two centuries, Near Eastern archaeologists have excavated large public structures, including fortifications, temples, and palaces; many tens of thousands of tombs; and just as many private dwellings, some no more than campsites. Each one of these locales, if properly excavated, contains all sorts of evidence, much of which may be relevant to the Bible. This evidence includes material enabling dating of the locale by scientific or typological means; remains of the flora and fauna used by the inhabitants; artifacts, or fragments of artifacts, in materials such as stone, ceramics, metal, wood, and glass; and sometimes inscriptions and texts, including many discussed in this chapter and elsewhere in this book.

On a broad scale, the discovery, excavation, and dating of fortifications and monumental buildings, for example, help fill in gaps in what the Bible and nonbiblical texts say. The presence of imported artifacts makes it possible to determine imperial control and trade patterns. On a more mundane level, excavated small finds enable us to reconstruct elements of daily life: tools, diet, clothing, social structure and stratification, and so on.[12]

Here are three examples of how archaeological data and the Bible intersect, with a focus on the First Temple in Jerusalem. According to 1 Kings, among King Solomon's other public works were the refortification of several cities, including "Jerusalem, Hazor, Megiddo, and Gezer" (9:14). Excavating at the site of Hazor in northern Galilee in the 1950s, archaeologists uncovered a six-chambered four-entryway gate, which they dated to the tenth century BCE, when Solomon was king (see Figure 5.1). Gates with the same design and almost the same size were also uncovered at Megiddo and Gezer. Although a majority of scholars date all three gate complexes to the tenth century BCE because of the ceramics associated with them, a substantial minority think that they should be dated a century or so later. One other piece of evidence is relevant. The prophet Ezekiel, who had been a priest in the Temple in Jerusalem before he was taken into exile in Babylonia in 597 BCE, describes a vision of Jerusalem and the Temple restored. In the vision of the future Temple, largely based on the Temple in which he had served as a priest, he describes the gates of the Temple compound having three recesses on either side—in other words, a six-chambered four-entryway gate.[13] Thus,

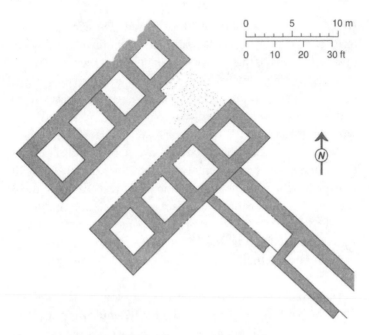

Figure 5.1 A tenth-century BCE gate at Hazor.

archaeological data and biblical sources have at least a rough
convergence, even if questions of date remain.

A second example has to do with the plan of Solomon's
royal quarter, which included the Temple and the palace, described in 1 Kings 6. Like other temples in the region in same
period, Solomon's Temple had a longitudinal axis. A portico
led to three inner rooms, the rearmost of which was the most
sacred area. At Tell Tayinat in southern Turkey, one temple of
this design was attached to a much larger royal complex; another was nearby (see Figure 5.2). Although Solomon's Temple
took seven years to build, the construction of the royal quarter
took almost twice as long,[14] so that, as at Tayinat, the Temple
was more like a royal chapel than a large public building (see
Figure 5.3).

A third example has to do with the most sacred Israelite
ritual object, the divine throne in the innermost room of the

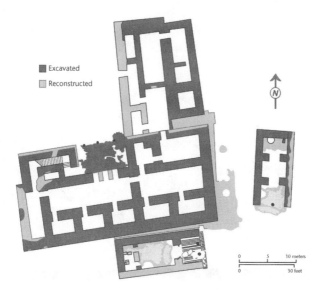

Figure 5.2 The royal complex at Tell Tayinat.

Temple. At Megiddo, in northwestern Israel, archaeologists in the 1930s found an ivory plaque (see Figure 5.4). The carved ivory, which is about ten inches long, depicts sequential scenes. On the right, a king in a chariot is returning victorious from battle. Ahead of him, a soldier leads two naked circumcised captives. Three lotus plants divide this scene from the one on the left, where the same king is seated on his throne, celebrating his victory. He holds a lotus in his left hand and is drinking from a bowl in his right. He is attended by a woman, directly in front of him, probably the queen, behind whom is a woman playing a lyre. At the far left, the king's servants are mixing wine for the king. Of special interest for our purposes here is the king's throne. Its side is a winged sphinx, and his feet are resting on a footstool.

A throne of the same design is depicted in a relief on the sarcophagus of Ahiram, king of Byblos, a Phoenician city north of Beirut, dating to about 1000 BCE and excavated in 1923 (see Figure 5.5). We see a king, presumably Ahiram himself, seated

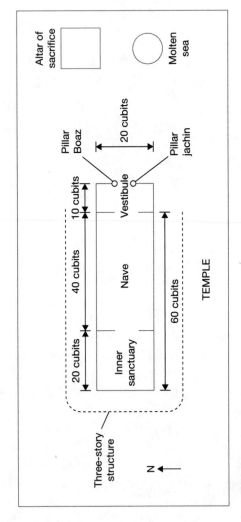

Figure 5.3 Solomon's Temple.

Figure 5.4 An ivory plaque from Megiddo.
Courtesy of the Oriental Institute of the University of Chicago

Figure 5.5 The Ahiram sarcophagus.
Erich Lessing / Art Resource, NY

on a sphinx-sided throne, his feet on a footstool, holding a cup in his right hand and, again, a lotus blossom in his left hand—but this time the lotus is drooping, probably symbolizing his death. In a procession, courtiers bring the deceased king various offerings, presumably for the funerary rituals.

The divine throne in Solomon's Temple in Jerusalem is similar to these depictions. Its sides were the cherubim, composite creatures like sphinxes.[15] The Bible often speaks of the god of Israel as "enthroned on the cherubim"; for example,

> The LORD, enthroned on cherubim, is king,
>   peoples tremble, the earth quakes. . . .
> Exalt the LORD our God,
>   and bow down to His footstool. (Psalm 99:1, 5,
>   New Jewish Publication Society Translation)[16]

So, like the thrones on the Megiddo ivory and the Ahiram sarcophagus, the LORD's throne had a footstool, frequently called "the ark of the covenant."[17] All of this and much other archaeological evidence enables us to reconstruct the First Temple and its furnishings.

The ark of the covenant must have been among the spoils that the Babylonians took from the Temple when they destroyed Jerusalem in 586 BCE, although it is not explicitly mentioned in catalogues of those spoils.[18] That omission inspired the development of a later legend that the prophet Jeremiah removed the ark and other sacred objects and deposited them in a cave on Mount Nebo, where Moses had died.[19] Despite occasional searches, however, the lost ark has never been found, except in fiction and in film.

Does archaeology prove the Bible?

Neither the Bible nor other texts are completely reliable guides to interpreting excavated material. Just as geography provides the scenery, archaeology provides the set, the props, and the like. It is better to think of archaeological data and biblical (and nonbiblical) texts as separate kinds of evidence, both of which need to be interpreted. If the interpretation of archaeological data and the interpretation of biblical texts do not agree, then the interpretations need to be reconsidered: The evidence is what it is.

Only rarely is there a direct, one-to-one correlation between archaeological data and something in the Bible. Here is an often-cited example. In Jerusalem, there is a 1,750-foot-long tunnel under the oldest part of the city, known as the City of David, through which water flows from the spring Gihon on the eastern side of the city to its southwestern side. According to 2 Chronicles, "Hezekiah closed the upper outlet of the waters of Gihon and directed them down to the west side of the city of David" (32:30; see also 2 Kings 20:20). In the late eighth century BCE, Hezekiah, the king of Judah, was preparing for an expected attack on Jerusalem by the Assyrian king Sennacherib, because Hezekiah had withheld the required tribute. Part of the preparation involved redirecting the city's water supply from the spring, where it was vulnerable, to the newly fortified western side. In 1880, a boy swimming in the tunnel discovered a large inscription in Hebrew near the tunnel's western outlet. It describes how two teams of workers, coming from opposite directions, met in the center; the now-incomplete inscription reads in part:

> While there were still three cubits to tunnel through, the voice of a man was heard calling out to his co-worker, because there was a fissure in the rock, running from south to north. And on the final day of tunneling, each of the stonecutters was striking the stone forcefully so as to meet his co-worker, pick after pick. And then the water began to flow from the source to the pool, a distance of 1,200 cubits. And 100 cubits was the height of the rock above the head of the stonecutters.[20]

Almost all scholars agree that the tunnel, and its inscription, relate to the biblical description of Hezekiah's redirection of the city's water supply. But the inscription commemorates the workers' accomplishment and does not mention Hezekiah, and the biblical texts do not explicitly mention a tunnel, so there is not absolute correspondence between the biblical and the archaeological evidence. This has allowed a few scholars to suggest alternate views.[21]

One archaeological site often cited, especially in conservative circles, as proving that the Bible is historically accurate is that of the ancient city of Jericho (modern Tell es-Sultan), just northwest of the Dead Sea. An excavator of the site in the 1930s, John Garstang, dated walls that had been destroyed and burned to the fifteenth century BCE, and connected this destruction with the biblical account in Joshua 6 of Jericho's wall falling down and causing the city's destruction. In her re-excavation of the site in the 1950s, however, Kathleen Kenyon redated the same walls a thousand years earlier, long before the time of Joshua. Now, almost all scholars agree that in the time when Joshua likely lived (late thirteenth to early twelfth century BCE, presuming of course that he was an actual historical person), Jericho was uninhabited. Still, some conservative commentators claim that Garstang's results proved that the book of Joshua was literally and historically true.[22] Similar claims are made for others of the many cities that Joshua is reported to have destroyed. But neither at Jericho nor elsewhere is there any memorial that states, in effect, "Joshua destroyed this city." So archaeology does not "prove" anything about the book of Joshua's account of the Israelite conquest of Canaan.

6

INTERPRETIVE STRATEGIES

What are interpretive strategies?

Interpretive strategies are methodologies of various types used in studying the Bible. Some of these, such as textual criticism and archaeology, we have discussed earlier, and some, such as reception history, we will discuss in subsequent chapters. Many of them overlap, and all can be useful in the process of interpretation.

What is a concordance?

A basic interpretive strategy is using a concordance. A concordance is an alphabetical list of all the words (or the most important words) in a major work or a body of literature and where precisely they occur. So, there are concordances to the works of Homer and Shakespeare, of Emily Dickinson and James Joyce, and, of course, to the Bible.

For the Bible, a concordance is an invaluable resource to use when studying the meanings of a word or the development of a concept. The first concordances to the Bible were produced in the Middle Ages, and until the late twentieth century they were compiled, painstakingly, by hand. Now, with the development of computers, electronic concordances are relatively easy to produce and can be used in more complex searches. Readily available online are concordances for the Hebrew and Aramaic of the Hebrew Bible, for the Greek both of the Septuagint and of the New Testament, and for translations into English and other languages both ancient and modern.

Sometimes using a concordance of a translation can be misleading. For example, in the Hebrew Bible there are two frequently used different words for "covenant," *berit* and *edut* (from different sources; see pages 87–88). Both ancient and modern translators have not always distinguished between them; for example, the New Revised Standard Version (NRSV) translates both as "covenant," but for the second usually has a textual note giving the alternatives of "treaty" and "testimony."[1]

What is source criticism?

Source criticism is the investigation of the works authors may have used as a basis for their own works. Source criticism is widely used in comparative literature: A source critic might study how in *The Comedy of Errors*, Shakespeare adapted the Roman dramatist Plautus's *Menaechmi* (a play about twins separated when young, and both named Menaechmus), or how the French dramatist Racine used the biblical book of Kings for his tragedy *Athalie*.[2]

In biblical studies, the sources investigated may be actual, like the already-existing books of Samuel and Kings used by the author of Chronicles, or hypothetical, like the possible sources of the Pentateuch and the Gospels.

How does source criticism work in the Torah/Pentateuch?

With few exceptions, in Jewish and Christian tradition until the Enlightenment, Moses was believed to have been the writer, if not necessarily the ultimate author, of all of the Torah/Pentateuch. In the seventeenth century, however, some Jewish and Christian thinkers began to look at those first five books of the Bible without theological presuppositions. Among other things, they observed that those books have a large number of repetitions and inconsistencies, which one would not ordinarily expect from a single author, whether human or divine. For example, in the story of the Flood, *God* first tells Noah to bring two of every kind of birds and animals into the ark, male and female, but immediately after that, *the* LORD tells him to bring "seven pairs of all clean animals . . . and a pair of the animals that are not clean" (Genesis 6:19–20; 7:2–3). As this example also shows, especially in the book of Genesis there is a bewildering variation in the names used for God. In some parts, God is simply called *God* (Hebrew *elohim*); in others, he is called *Yahweh* (traditionally translated "the LORD").[3]

Using these and other criteria, scholars began to divide the Pentateuch into separate sources or "documents," a process that culminated in the classic formulation by the German scholar Julius Wellhausen of the "Documentary Hypothesis" in 1878. In this hypothetical reconstruction, underlying the current text of the Pentateuch are four separate sources or documents with distinctive styles and features, here summarized in chronological order:

- J (from German Jahweh = English Yahweh, usually translated "the LORD"), which predominantly uses the divine name Yahweh, especially in Genesis, and which Wellhausen dated to the tenth century BCE. Many of the familiar stories in the early chapters of Genesis are assigned to this source, including those of the second account of creation and the Garden of Eden, Cain and Abel, one version of the Flood, and the Tower of Babel.
- E, which predominantly uses the divine name *elohim* (usually translated "God"), especially in Genesis, dated to the eighth century BCE. One famous story assigned to this source is that of Abraham's near-sacrifice of Isaac in Genesis 22.
- D, found almost exclusively in the book of Deuteronomy, which usually uses the divine name Yahweh, dated to the seventh century BCE (see further pages 58–59).

- P, the Priestly source, which emphasizes matters of ritual and purity and also predominantly uses the divine name *elohim*, especially in Genesis, dated to the sixth century BCE. The first account of creation in Genesis 1 and an alternate version of the Flood story are examples of narratives assigned to this source.

Each of these sources was composed and compiled in different historical contexts by writers with different perspectives and different theologies. This source criticism is often misleadingly called "literary criticism," although it only loosely fits the usual sense of that term.

As the name "Documentary Hypothesis" itself indicates, this theory is hypothetical in the sense that none of these documents has ever been found, but, like scientific hypotheses, it helps explain the many confusing features of the Pentateuch. The Documentary Hypothesis dominated Pentateuchal studies from the late nineteenth to the late twentieth centuries by most Protestant scholars except the most conservative, and by the mid-twentieth century many Jewish and most Roman Catholic scholars were using it as well. In recent decades, however, it has repeatedly been challenged, and what had been a broad scholarly consensus has now somewhat dissipated. Still, it remains the indispensable starting point for the study of the Pentateuch.

Is source criticism used in studying other parts of the Hebrew Bible?

Yes. Many of the historical books, and sometimes others as well, give as kind of footnotes the sources their authors used in creating them. These sources are seldom extant, but parallels in other cultures make it relatively easy to determine their nature. Thus, the book of Kings repeatedly refers to "the Book of the Annals of the Kings of Israel" and "the Book of the Annals of the Kings of Judah"; although these ancient archives no longer exist, Egyptian and Mesopotamian parallels do. Other no-longer-surviving sources mentioned by biblical writers include two poetic collections, "the Book of the Wars of Yahweh" (Numbers 21:14) and "the Book of Jashar" (Joshua 10:13; 2 Samuel 1:18), as well as prophetic collections such as "the records of the seer Samuel, and . . . the records of the prophet Nathan, and . . . the records of the seer Gad" (1 Chronicles 29:29).

Most informative is comparing the book of Chronicles with its sources that have survived. The author of Chronicles, writing in the fifth or fourth century BCE, had access to many already-existing biblical books or at least their substance, such as Genesis, Psalms, and especially Samuel and Kings. In retelling the history of the Israelite monarchies in 1 Chronicles 10 to 2 Chronicles 36, the Chronicler often borrowed from Samuel and Kings, sometimes copying chapter after chapter (ancient ideas about plagiarism were different from ours!). When we compare the earlier and later works, looking for what the Chronicler deleted and added, we learn that writer's purpose and point of view.[4]

Similar insights are gained by comparing the versions of events described elsewhere in the Bible and their recapitulation in the so-called historical psalms, such as the accounts of the lives of Israel's ancestors and the Exodus from Egypt in Psalms 105 and 106, and of creation and the Exodus in Psalm 136.

How does source criticism work in the Gospels?

The Synoptic Gospels, Matthew, Mark, and Luke, are closely related. They have essentially the same plot and narrative chronology, and many passages are almost identical. Clearly they have some literary relationship to each other, as the example in Box 6.1 shows.

A majority of scholars, but by no means all, think that Mark was the earliest Gospel, and that the authors of Matthew and Luke independently used Mark as a source. But there are

---

BOX 6.1 Example of Synoptic parallels (King James Version)

Mark 10:13–16
And they brought young children to him, that he should touch them: and his disciples rebuked those that brought them. But when Jesus saw it, he was much displeased, and said unto them, "Suffer the little children to come unto me, and forbid them not: for of such is the kingdom of God. Verily I say unto you, Whosoever shall not receive the kingdom of God as a little child, he shall not enter therein." And he took them up in his arms, put his hands on them, and blessed them.

Matthew 19:13–15
Then there were brought unto him little children, that he should put his hands on them, and pray: and the disciples rebuked them. But Jesus said, "Suffer little children, and forbid them not, to come unto me: for of such is the kingdom of heaven." And he laid his hands on them, and departed thence.

Luke 18:15–17
And they brought unto him also infants, that he would touch them: but when his disciples saw it, they rebuked them. But Jesus called them unto him, and said, "Suffer little children to come unto me, and forbid them not: for of such is the kingdom of God. Verily I say unto you, Whosoever shall not receive the kingdom of God as a little child shall in no wise enter therein."[5]

---

passages in Matthew that have close parallels in Luke but are not found in Mark; for the most part these are sayings of Jesus, such as the Beatitudes (Matthew 5:3–12; Luke 6:20–23) and the Lord's Prayer (Matthew 6:9–13, Luke 12:2–4). Either Luke used Matthew as a source, or vice versa, or they both independently used another source. The third option has led many scholars to posit a hypothetical source known as Q (from German *Quelle*, "source"). This source, like those of the Documentary Hypothesis in the Pentateuch, does not exist, but, like a scientific hypothesis, it is a likely explanation of the data—that is, the often-verbatim parallel passages in Matthew and Luke that are not in Mark. Finally, there is material in both Matthew (such as the parable of the laborers in the vineyard, 20:1–16) and Luke (such as the parable of the good Samaritan, 10:30–37) not found in any other Gospel, so some scholars have also proposed that they each had one or more independent sources (called "M" and "L" respectively). The result of this source criticism looks like this:

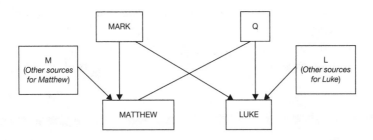

What preceded Q?

The hypothetical source Q was in Greek. But Jesus would have spoken to his audiences in Aramaic, so there must also have been an oral or written source from which Q was translated. That such a collection of sayings existed is suggested by other sayings of Jesus not found in the Gospels. For example, Acts 20:35 quotes Jesus saying: "It is more blessed to give than to receive"; this certainly sounds like something Jesus might have said.

We can see oral tradition at work when we examine the earliest account of Jesus's words at the Last Supper:

> For I received from the Lord what I also handed on to you, that the Lord Jesus on the night he was handed over, took bread, and, after he had given thanks, broke it and said, "This is my body that is for you. Do this in remembrance

of me." In the same way also the cup, after supper, saying, "This cup is the new covenant in my blood. Do this, as often as you drink it, in remembrance of me." (1 Corinthians 11:23–25, New American Bible, Revised Edition [NABRE])

Now Paul was not present at the Last Supper, nor had he ever known Jesus in person, so when he speaks of having received and handing on, he must be speaking of oral tradition. This is also the case when Paul refers to Jesus's teaching as "the word of the Lord" (1 Thessalonians 4:15; see also 1 Corinthians 7:10).

Comparing Jesus's words in the other accounts of the Last Supper is also instructive:

"Take it; this is my body." . . . "This is my blood of the covenant, which will be shed for many." (Mark 14:22–24, NABRE)

"Take and eat; this is my body." . . . "Drink from it, all of you, for this is my blood of the covenant, which will be shed on behalf of many for the forgiveness of sins." (Matthew 26:26–28, NABRE)

"Take this and share it among yourselves." . . . "This is my body, which will be given for you; do this in memory of me." . . . "This cup is the new covenant in my blood, which will be shed for you." (Luke 22:15–20, NABRE)

The variations in Jesus's words may be the result of oral traditions, or they may reflect the different formulations used in different early Christian churches, as is also the case in Christianity today. In any case, even for what became a central Christian ritual, exact quotation of what Jesus may have said does not seem to have mattered.

What is the Gospel of Thomas and why is it important?

The Gospel of Thomas, discovered in 1945 at Nag Hammadi in Egypt, provides further evidence for collections of sayings of Jesus. The Gospel of Thomas has 114 such sayings; although written in Coptic, they had been translated from Greek. Some of the sayings in the Gospel of Thomas are also found in the four canonical Gospels; others are known from quotations in early Christian writers and from modern manuscript discoveries. Dates proposed for the original Greek version of the Gospel of Thomas range from the mid-50s to the mid-second century CE. If the early date is correct, the Gospel of Thomas would provide a parallel to the hypothetical collection of sayings known as Q.

The Gospel of Thomas identifies its putative source and author in its introduction: "These are the secret sayings that the living Jesus spoke and Didymos Judas Thomas recorded."[6] "Didymos" is the Greek word for twin, and "Thomas" is derived from an Aramaic word with the same meaning. According to the Synoptic Gospels, Thomas was one of the Twelve, called "the Twin" in the Gospel of John,[7] and some noncanonical sources give Thomas's actual name as Judas. Whose twin Thomas was is not known, although a few scholars have proposed the fascinating—if theologically challenging for some—possibility that he was Jesus's own twin brother.[8]

It is unlikely, however, that the person responsible for this collection was the apostle Thomas. Nor, as is also the case with sayings of Jesus found in other Gospels, is Jesus likely to have spoken all of these sayings; here is an example of a saying that sounds unlike anything Jesus might have said:

Jesus said, "Lucky is the lion that the human will eat, so that the lion becomes human. And foul is the human that the lion will eat, and the lion still will become human." (7)

Another saying not found in the canonical Gospels that the Jesus Seminar[9] thought was probably from Jesus himself is the cryptic and abruptly ending parable of the empty jar:

> Jesus said, "The Father's kingdom is like a woman who was carrying a jar full of meal. While she was walking along a distant road, the handle of the jar broke and the meal spilled behind her on the road. She didn't know it; she hadn't noticed a problem. When she reached her house, she put her jar down and discovered that it was empty." (97)

How does the Gospel of John differ from the Synoptic Gospels, and why?

When we turn to the Gospel of John after reading the Synoptic Gospels, we find a very different work. Although Jesus, John the Baptist, Peter, Judas Iscariot, Mary Magdalene, Pontius Pilate, and a few other characters familiar from the Synoptic Gospels are all in John, many others are not. Even Mary the mother of Jesus is not named. And we meet several new characters, including Nathanael, Nicodemus, an unnamed Samaritan woman, and Lazarus.

Although the author of the Gospel of John was familiar with at least some of the Synoptic Gospels, or the sources that they used, its presentation of the life, teaching, death, and resurrection of Jesus differs from theirs in important ways. Whereas Jesus's active ministry in the Synoptics apparently lasts for less than a year, in John it is two or three years long.[10] In the Synoptics, Jesus enters the Temple and disrupts the money changers a few days before his death, while in John it occurs at the beginning of his ministry. In the Synoptics, Jesus's death takes place on the day following the Passover meal, while in John it takes place on the day before Passover, so in John the

Last Supper is not a Passover meal and Jesus's crucifixion occurs on the first day of Passover.

Only one of Jesus's miracles is found in all four Gospels, the feeding of five thousand; Jesus's walking on water is also found in Matthew, Mark, and John. Although all four Gospels have accounts of Jesus healing people and raising the dead, the characters in those miracle stories are different in the Synoptics and in John.

Just as significant as these differences is the content of Jesus's preaching in the Synoptic Gospels and in John. In the Synoptics, Jesus's message is primarily about the kingdom of God, both present and future, and how he wants his audience to relate to God and to each other. In John, Jesus speaks of "the kingdom of God" in only one context (3:3–5); in Matthew, which is only slightly longer than John, Jesus speaks of "the kingdom of heaven" (Matthew's equivalent to "the kingdom of God") more than thirty times. Many of these occurrences are in parables—a genre characteristic of Jesus's preaching, in which something from ordinary life is given a deeper meaning—but we find no parables as such in John. Moreover, few of the sayings of Jesus found in the Synoptics occur in John. Finally, while in the Synoptic Gospels Jesus speaks about himself only occasionally, in John most of the long speeches of Jesus have to do with his self-identification as God's son and the only access to God. "I am the way, and the truth, and the life. No one come to the Father except through me," Jesus reportedly says (John 14:6, NRSV; see also 3:35–36), and he expands on this in a series of first-person pronouncements, identifying himself as the bread of life, the light of the world, the good shepherd, and the resurrection and the life.[11]

Because of these differences, almost all scholars agree that John is the latest of the four Gospels, with a much more developed theology about who Jesus Christ was than that of the Synoptics.

What is form criticism?

Form criticism is a methodology developed in the early twentieth century by the German scholar Hermann Gunkel in his commentaries on the books of Genesis and Psalms. Gunkel sought to determine the genres—the "forms"—of smaller units in these books, such as legends, folktales, myths, genealogies, proverbs, hymns, and laments, and also how these "forms" would have functioned in their original social settings in ancient Israel. Since Gunkel, form criticism has been used in the interpretation of the entire Hebrew Bible and of the Apocrypha. Many of the genres found in those canonical units have also been found in nonbiblical writings. One important example is the international treaty, elements of which have been identified in biblical texts, such as the blessings and curses for covenant observance and violation found in Leviticus 26, Deuteronomy 28, and elsewhere.

Two of Gunkel's students, Martin Dibelius and Rudolf Bultmann, applied Gunkel's methodology to the New Testament, where genres such as sayings, parables, infancy narratives, miracle stories, passion narratives, and resurrection narratives have been identified and studied in relationship both to the life of Jesus and to their uses in early Christianity, as well as in comparison with the uses of those genres in other biblical and nonbiblical literatures.

What are infancy narratives and how can they be interpreted?

Infancy narratives are legendary stories about the conception, birth, and early childhood of heroic figures. Such narratives are found in many literatures, for example about such heroes as Romulus and Remus, George Washington, and Superman. In the Bible, we find examples of infancy narratives about Isaac, Samson, Samuel, and John the Baptist, all born to women apparently unable to have children, and about Moses, rescued from infanticide by his resourceful mother and sister. Such stories inform readers that from the outset, those individuals were divinely favored or destined for greatness.

Both Matthew 1–2 and Luke 1–2 drew on these and other biblical and nonbiblical accounts in writing their narratives about Jesus's early life. Furthermore, although in Christian retellings and artistic representations of the Christmas story the two narratives are combined, for the most part they are very different. In Matthew, only Joseph receives divine messages from unnamed angels, although he never speaks himself; in Luke, the angel Gabriel appears only to Mary, who speaks repeatedly. The familiar wise men and the flight into Egypt are found only in Matthew; the visit of the shepherds occurs only in Luke. In Matthew, Jesus is born in a house in Bethlehem, apparently his parents' home; in Luke he is born in a stable in Bethlehem, where his parents had traveled from Nazareth to register for a census. In fact, the only details the two narratives have in common are Jesus's conception by the virgin Mary, her husband Joseph, and Jesus's birth in Bethlehem.

That a virgin could give birth to the son of a god would not have seemed impossible to readers in the Greco-Roman world, where various heroes of mythology had mixed human and divine parentage. Like such myths, the virgin birth of Jesus is a matter of belief, not of history. It also seems to have developed relatively late in earliest Christianity. It is not found in the earliest books of the New Testament: not in Paul's letters,[12] nor in the earliest Gospel, Mark, which tells us nothing about Jesus before his adulthood.

Rather, the virgin birth of Jesus, like many other details in the infancy narratives of Matthew and Luke, is a kind of theological fiction intended to elaborate the belief that in Jesus, Christians can see the fulfillment of the Jewish scriptures. Matthew tells us as much: "All this took place to fulfil what had been spoken by the Lord through the prophet: 'Look, the virgin shall conceive and bear a son'" (1:22–23). Matthew uses this "fulfillment formula" about a dozen times in his Gospel, including four times in his infancy narrative. For Matthew,

Jesus is simultaneously a new Moses, rescued as an infant from an evil king's death warrant; a new Israel, like Israel of old going down to Egypt and then returning to the Promised Land; and a new David, like him from Bethlehem.[13]

Luke's use of the Jewish scriptures is similar. Like some childless mothers in the Hebrew Bible, both Elizabeth and Mary eventually have sons. Mary thanks God for her pregnancy in a poetic prayer derived in part from that of Hannah, Samuel's mother,[14] and the narrative also alludes to the one about Sarah, Isaac's mother.

Matthew and Luke's infancy narratives thus tell us little about the historical Jesus, but a great deal about what early Christian writers believed about him. Later Christian writers created even more elaborate tales about Jesus's early life, as in *The Infancy Gospel of Thomas* and *The Proto-Gospel of James*.

What are the passion narratives and how can they be interpreted?

The passion narratives are the accounts in Matthew 26–27, Mark 14–15, Luke 22–23, and John 18–19 of the suffering (for which the Latin word is *passio*) and death of Jesus. Probably the most difficult theological problem that early Christians faced was how to reconcile their belief that Jesus was the Messiah with his execution by the Roman authorities in Judea. One way that they dealt with this cognitive dissonance was to develop the belief that Jesus would return in triumph to complete the Messiah's expected work. Another was to reconstruct in elaborate detail the events of his last days, in order to find meaning in them.

Sources for this reconstruction must have included oral traditions, based on eyewitness accounts, as Luke suggests in his prologue (1:2). Both the oral traditions and possibly also a written passion narrative based on them were sources for the Gospel writers. Certainly we find substantial agreement among the Gospels on the essential elements of the end of

Jesus's life, greater agreement than about the rest of his life. These include:

- Jesus's entry into Jerusalem;
- disruption of Temple activity;[15]
- plots by Jewish religious authorities to have Jesus killed;
- evening meal on the Thursday before Jesus's death;[16]
- betrayal by Judas Iscariot;
- prayer and arrest in a garden on the Mount of Olives;[17]
- cutting off the ear of a slave of the high priest;
- trials before various religious and civil authorities, including the Roman governor Pontius Pilate;
- Peter's denial that he knew Jesus;
- release of Barabbas;
- casting lots for his garments;
- crucifixion with two others at Golgotha;
- the presence of women followers of Jesus as witnesses to his death.

These multiple attestations suggest that at least some of the elements are probably historically accurate. At the same time, the Gospel writers separately add details to this shared tradition. Because they believed that in Jesus the Jewish scriptures had been fulfilled—in fact, John 12:41 says that the prophet Isaiah was speaking about Jesus—those scriptures were used as another source for accounts of his life and especially of his suffering, death, and resurrection, much as they were for accounts of his birth and early childhood. Many of the details are derived from three biblical texts, Psalms 22 and 69 and Isaiah 53: The passion narratives in the Gospels contain five quotations from these texts and more than two dozen allusions to them. The historical accuracy of such details is thus often questionable.

We are given a clue about this in the report of Jesus praying while he was on the cross, using the opening verse of Psalm 22: "My God, my God! Why have you forsaken me?" The original psalmist goes on to report to God that his suffering includes being mocked by others, thirst, and his enemies casting lots for his clothing; all of these elements are either quoted or alluded to in the Gospels. For example, John reports that the Roman soldiers crucifying Jesus cast lots for his tunic, which was unusually seamless, because, as John puts it, "This was to fulfill what the scripture says, 'They divided my clothes among themselves, and for my clothing they cast lots'" (19:24, quoting Psalm 22:18).[18]

The Gospel passion narratives also drew on biblical and nonbiblical stories about how prophets and other heroic figures suffered and died.[19] Later writers combined the Gospel accounts with others in such apocryphal works as the *Gospel of Peter* and the *Gospel of Nicodemus*, which includes the "Acts of Pilate," in the Christian liturgy for Holy Week, and in medieval mystery plays.

What is tradition criticism?

Tradition criticism (also known as tradition-historical criticism) is the study of the larger oral and written components underlying a biblical book. Tradition critics seek to determine what the original form of these components may have been, and how they were adapted in the course of their transmission and incorporation into the final text. For example, a cycle of stories, such as those about David, that originated in one historical context could be shaped in order to fit in another later one. Tradition criticism is mainly used by scholars of the Hebrew Bible/Old Testament, while New Testament scholars more characteristically use redaction criticism. Methodologically they are very similar.

What is redaction criticism?

Redaction criticism, which closely resembles tradition criticism, is the study of how the editors of many biblical books—the "redactors"—combined various sources, both oral and written, to produce their final form. Redaction criticism aims to get at what the editors were trying to communicate. So, redaction critics will study the Gospel of Luke, to see how its use and arrangement of material from Q, from Mark, and from L contributes to its presentation of the theological significance of Jesus's life, teaching, death, and resurrection for Luke's early Christian audience.

Although redaction criticism was originally applied only to the Gospels, more recently it has been applied to the Hebrew Bible, the Apocrypha, and some of the other books of the New Testament as well. It also overlaps both with tradition criticism (see page 100) and canonical criticism (see pages 103–4). Here is an example that shows this overlap. The book of Isaiah has a complex literary history, the initial stages of which are indicated in the book itself. Early in the book the prophet, speaking in the first person, instructs an unidentified person (perhaps a scribe) to "Bind up the testimony, seal the teaching among my disciples" (8:16), meaning that the prophet's words are to be written down "so that it may be for the time to come, as a witness forever" (30:8). The first stage in the formation of the book, then, was that the prophet's sayings (scholars often call them oracles) were written down and collected. These sayings were then edited by others, like the "disciples" just mentioned, who added to them editorial notes and third-person narratives about the eighth-century prophet Isaiah. This collection was then expanded; thus we find in Isaiah 36–39 a prose account of the Assyrian attack on Jerusalem in 701 BCE taken from 2 Kings 18–20.

In the late nineteenth century, scholars recognized that chapters 40–66 of the book of Isaiah seem to come from a later time than that described in chapters 1–39. In the earlier part, Judah's primary enemy is Assyria; in the subsequent part, it is Babylon. The first part mentions eighth-century BCE rulers known from biblical and nonbiblical sources; the second mentions the Persian king Cyrus, of the mid-sixth century BCE.

Because of these and other differences, most scholars now think that Isaiah 40–55, although using some of the same vocabulary and themes as Isaiah 1–39, was written over a century later, by an anonymous writer belonging to a kind of "school of Isaiah" analogous to schools of Greek philosophy. To this "Second Isaiah," scholars further think, was later added "Third Isaiah," chapters 56–66. Redaction criticism focuses on how these various stages were combined.

What is the Deuteronomistic History?

Another example of how tradition criticism and redaction criticism overlap is the Deuteronomistic History, identified as the books of Joshua, Judges, Samuel, and Kings. The identification of this larger unit was made by the German scholar Martin Noth in the 1940s. Observing that these books often shared vocabulary, style, and point of view with the book of Deuteronomy, Noth proposed that there was something like a Deuteronomic school that both produced the book of Deuteronomy and then, using it as a kind of theological preface, constructed a history of Israel in the Promised Land, from its conquest by Joshua to the Babylonian destruction of Jerusalem in 586 BCE. For the authors of Deuteronomy and the Deuteronomistic History, the Israelites' successes and failures are a direct result of their obedience or disobedience to the teaching of Moses. The final stage of this work was therefore written after 586 BCE, although there seem to have been one or more earlier stages as well, both for Deuteronomy and the Deuteronomistic History itself. Redaction criticism examines the earlier and final stages of composition, while tradition-historical criticism examines how the historians used earlier oral and written sources to compile their work. Some of these sources are named (see pages 88–89), and some are hypothetical, such as the Succession History of David, proposed for 2 Samuel 9–1 Kings 2.

The theory of the Deuteronomistic History has the effect of severing the book of Deuteronomy from the preceding four books of the Torah/Pentateuch, which means that the original endings of the Pentateuch's other hypothetical sources have been lost.

What is canonical criticism?

Another methodology that focuses on the final form of a text is canonical criticism. Canonical criticism first focuses on the canon itself as it has functioned in Christianity. Canonical critics argue that the individual books of the Bible are best interpreted when viewing the Bible as a whole, a unified work, in other words, as sacred scripture, which is how it was read for most of Christian history. Canonical criticism thus intersects with theology.

A subset of canonical criticism is the examination of a particular book in its canonical final form as a unified work. Examples of books for which this has been attempted are Psalms and the Book of the Twelve Minor Prophets.

One critique of canonical criticism is that it must choose among the several canons of the Bible. The Hebrew Bible, the Tanakh, does not include the Apocrypha or the New Testament, and its books are in a different order than those of the Protestant canon, which also does not include the Apocrypha as Roman Catholic and Orthodox canons do. Moreover, for many centuries, the canon of Western Christianity was the Latin translation known as the Vulgate, and that of Eastern Christianity (for the Old Testament) has been the Septuagint. In the treatment of smaller units, their canonical form often was not set until relatively late; thus, for example, the order of the Major Prophets, and also that of the Minor Prophets, varies in some sources, although each division is generally in roughly chronological order.

What are cultural and ideological criticisms?

Cultural and ideological criticisms interpret the Bible from specific social and political locations, such as gender, ethnicity, class, and nationality. These include—in alphabetical order, so as not to suggest that some are more valid than others—African-American criticism, Asian-American criticism, disability criticism, ecological criticism, Latino/Latina/Latinx criticisms, postcolonial criticism, queer criticism, trauma criticism, and womanist criticism, to name just a few.

What other methods do scholars use in interpreting the Bible?

Other methods are often adapted from other academic disciplines. So biblical scholars often use anthropology, economics, folklore, psychoanalysis, and sociology, again to name just a few. There are also interpretive strategies from the study of literature, including deconstructionism, performance criticism, postmodernism, reader-response criticism, rhetorical criticism, semiotics, and structuralism and poststructuralism.

Some scholars specialize in one approach, and I have learned much from them. I prefer to be eclectic, using whatever methods help me find new insights into texts I have studied for many years. But my starting point is always historical criticism: what a text meant to its original authors and audiences, insofar as we can know this.

7

THE USES OF THE BIBLE

What is reception history?

Reception history is a scholarly term for what we could call the study of the afterlives of the Bible: how, since it was being formed, the Bible has been used, from popular culture to high art. Such cultural influence of canonical works is not restricted to the Bible. To take two examples, over the ages Homer's *Iliad* and *Odyssey* have inspired innumerable works of literature, art, and music, as have the plays of Shakespeare.

For the Bible, we have commentaries and sermons by Jewish and Christian scholars from the beginning of the Common Era to the present. We also have the liturgical use of parts of the Bible in lectionaries, hymns, and prayers. We have poetry and fiction, and religious and secular art and music, drama, and dance. We have Handel's *Messiah* and the reggae hit "By the Rivers of Babylon." We have mosaics, medieval books of hours, and contemporary graphic novels. We have Michelangelo's *Moses* and Moses depicted on reliefs inside and outside the US Supreme Court. We have Cecil B. DeMille's *The Ten Commandments* and the Coen brothers' *A Serious Man*. And so on.

Such tracing of the cultural influence of the Bible requires expertise not only in the biblical sources, but also in the various genres influenced by the sources. Few scholars have such multiple expertise, but that has not stopped them from trying. An ongoing project is *The Encyclopedia of the Bible and Its Reception* (*EBR*), of which about two-thirds of the thirty projected volumes have appeared.[1]

What is the reception history of the book of Job?

I will sample the many media in which the reception history of the Bible is operative by focusing on the book of Job.[2] The reception history of the book of Job begins in the Bible itself. Job himself is an apparently well-known figure from folklore, linked with Noah and Danel, two other righteous heroes, in Ezekiel.[3] Job is also mentioned briefly in Sirach 49:9 and in James 5:11. In the ancient Greek translation of the Bible, the Septuagint, the book of Job is significantly shorter than in the Masoretic Text, although it also has two major additions, expanding the speech of Job's unnamed wife in 2:9 and the editorial conclusion in 42:17. Moreover, the Septuagint softens what its translators thought was apparently blasphemous language about God, translates "sons of God" as "angels,"[4] calls the mysterious "satan" of chapters 1 and 2 "the devil," and makes other changes that reflect the translators' own theology.

After an introduction and discussion of the book itself in the Hebrew Bible/Old Testament, *EBR*'s thirty-five-page entry on "Job (Book and Person)" has essays by different scholars on the book's reception history under the following headings and subheadings: New Testament; Judaism (Second Temple and Hellenistic Judaism; Rabbinic Judaism; Medieval Judaism; Modern Judaism); Christianity (Patristic to Modern Era; World Christianity); Islam; Other Religions; Literature; Visual Arts (Early Christian; Medieval Christian; Medieval Jewish; Medieval Islamic; Renaissance and Beyond); Music; Film; Dance. Each of these sections is essentially an annotated list, but given the vastness of the subject even for this one biblical book, also a necessarily incomplete one. For example, the section on Visual Arts lists in its bibliography the important study by Samuel Terrien, *The Iconography of Job Through the*

Centuries: Artists as Biblical Interpreters,[5] but can name only a small percentage of the works of art treated by Terrien. The Literature section is especially thin, omitting among others not only *Job: A Comedy of Justice* (1984), by the American science-fiction writer and novelist Robert A. Heinlein, but also the controversial *The Torments of Job* (1981), by the Israeli playwright Hanoch Levin. My pointing out these omissions is not meant to be negative, but simply to show how difficult and necessarily incomplete reception history can be.

In addition to this main entry, *EBR* has five more entries (in some seventeen pages) directly connected to the book of Job: Job, Targums of; Job, Testament of; Job's Daughters, International Order of (a Masonic subsidiary); Job's Friends; and Job's Wife.

One could do the same with every book of the Bible (and *EBR* eventually will!). Or one could narrow the focus considerably, as Susan Gillingham has done in her several-hundred-page study of the reception history of Psalms 1 and 2.[6] Gillingham herself, not entirely facetiously, has called reception history "biblical studies on holiday."[7]

How have people tried to edit the Bible?

Apart from scholarly commentaries, sometimes with in-text glosses (see Figures 2.1 and 2.2), which have existed from as early as the Dead Sea Scrolls to the present, over the ages new editions of the Bible or of parts of it have been produced that eliminated vocabulary, stories, and concepts that were thought to be theologically or otherwise erroneous or objectionable. Actually, the phenomenon of rewriting authoritative texts begins in the Bible itself. The author of the book of Chronicles, when retelling David's story, used the books of Samuel as a source. But although the Chronicler often copied that source verbatim, the Chronicler omitted the accounts of David's early life, including his battle with the Philistine giant Goliath, and when describing David's rule as king of Israel simply dropped unsavory episodes such as his affair with Bathsheba and his son Absalom's revolt. Moreover, although according to 2 Samuel 24:1 it was the LORD who incited David to take a census, in 1 Chronicles 21:1 it was "Satan." Similarly, in the New Testament, a majority of scholars think that the authors of Matthew and Luke expanded and corrected one of their sources, the Gospel of Mark.

Ancient translators did the same. Although the Hebrew text of the book of Esther never explicitly mentions God, in the ancient Greek translation, the Septuagint, at least some of which is probably based on a different Hebrew original, God is mentioned repeatedly. We find similar pious revisions in the Septuagint of the book of Job.

The second-century CE Christian scholar Marcion restricted the canonical scriptures to an abridged version of the Gospel of Luke, which has not survived, and the letters of Paul (excluding 1 and 2 Timothy, Titus, and Hebrews), who he thought was the only authentic apostle. The Old Testament was rejected, because in Marcion's view, it was the revelation not from the god who was Jesus's father, but from another, lesser, creator god. Not surprisingly, Marcion's views were viewed as heretical by most Christian authorities.

A similar approach, although for different reasons, was adopted by Thomas Jefferson. By literally cutting and pasting the King James Version, he harmonized the four Gospels into a single version, *The Life and Morals of Jesus of Nazareth* (completed in 1820, but not published until 1904). As a rationalist, Jefferson removed from the Gospels all miracles and supernatural events and persons. Thus, the Jefferson Bible ends with the burial of Jesus:

Now in the place where he was crucified there was a garden; and in the garden, a new sepulchre, wherein was never man yet laid. There laid they Jesus, and rolled a great stone to the door of the sepulchre, and departed.

The pious lexicographer Noah Webster (1758–1843) rewrote the King James Version (KJV) to update its language and to remove what he called "objectionable words and phrases . . . which cannot now be uttered, especially in promiscuous company, without violence to decency,"[8] because he thought that purity of language protected purity of mind. Sometimes Webster used what we might call hypereuphemisms, in which the biblical writers' own euphemisms are further obscured; for example, one of the curses for violation of covenant is that a woman will eat "her young one that cometh out from between her feet" (Deuteronomy 28:57; "feet" is a common biblical euphemism for the genitals); Webster changed this to "her young one, her own offspring." Similarly, in a speech by the Assyrian king Sennacherib's envoy to King Hezekiah's officials during the siege of Jerusalem in 701, the envoy says he has been sent to speak to the ordinary people observing the exchange: "Hath he not sent me to the men which sit upon the wall, that they may eat their own dung and drink their own piss" (2 Kings 18:27); Webster changes the last phrases to "that they may feed on their vilest excretions." And for the KJV's "who pisseth against the wall," a literal translation of a Hebrew phrase used only in curses, Webster has "male" (as do also the New Revised Standard Version [NRSV]; New Jewish Publication Society Translation [NJPS]; New American Bible, Revised Edition [NABRE]; and, usually, Common English Bible).[9]

Versions of the Bible for children have followed similar patterns. Moralizing additions are frequent in children's Bibles, and, unsurprisingly, biblical narratives having to do with sex and violence, both divine and human, are usually left out as inappropriate for children.

How has the Bible been used in liturgical services?

Readings from the Bible have been part of Jewish and Christian worship since late biblical times. Despite its canonical status, however, neither in Judaism nor in Christianity is the entire Bible read; for example, the theologically challenging books of Job and Ecclesiastes are seldom used in liturgical settings, and usually only extracts from these texts are read aloud (with the exception for Booths noted below).

In Jewish tradition, the entire Torah is read through annually in synagogue worship. The importance of the Torah in Jewish life is symbolized by making the "ark" in which the sacred handwritten Torah scrolls are stored the visual focus of the synagogue or temple. The daily portion from the Torah is followed on the Sabbath and major holy days by selections from the (Former and Latter) Prophets (*haftarah*). Also, on some major holy days individual books are read in their entirety: Esther on Purim, the Song of Solomon on Passover (Pesach), Ruth on Weeks (Shavuot), Lamentations on Tisha B'Av, and Ecclesiastes on Booths (Sukkot).

Many Christian denominations have assigned weekly or daily liturgical reading selections from the scriptures in "Lectionaries." Often these selections are keyed to the events commemorated on the major holy days; at other times a partial attempt is made to systematically cover the books of the Bible, but seldom is a complete book covered, not even the Gospels.

In both Jewish and Christian services, sermons are often given based on the readings from scripture. Psalms are also frequently chanted and recited, and other hymns and prayers from the scriptures or based on them are ubiquitous. One frequent prayer in both Jewish and Christian worship is the "Priestly Blessing":

> The LORD bless thee, and keep thee:
> The LORD make his face to shine upon thee, and be gracious unto thee:
> The LORD lift up his countenance upon thee, and give thee peace.
> (Numbers 6:24–26, KJV)

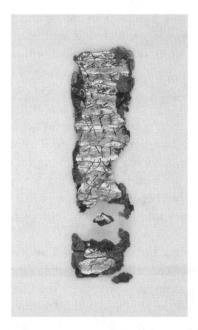

Figure 7.1 A silver plaque with a version of the Priestly Blessing, about 1.5 inches high.
Photo © The Israel Museum, Jerusalem by Ardon Bar-Hama

In a burial cave near Jerusalem dating to ca. 600 BCE and excavated in 1979, archaeologists found two rolled silver plaques used as amulets (see Figure 7.1). Written on the amulets were slightly variant versions of this blessing; these are the oldest texts so far discovered that became scriptural. Whether the amulets were keepsakes buried with their owners or prayers for the deceased after their death is impossible to say, but they show that the Priestly Blessing has been in continuous use for more than 2,600 years.[10]

Which Jewish holy days are based on the Bible?

The principal Jewish holy days are directly based on the Torah, and connected with events recounted in its narrative. These include the festivals of Unleavened Bread/Passover

(Pesach), originally linked with the spring barley harvest; Weeks (Shavuot), originally linked with the wheat harvest; and Booths (Sukkot), originally linked with the fall harvest of olives, grapes, and other produce. Each of these originally agricultural pilgrimage festivals was secondarily linked with the Exodus from Egypt: Passover commemorates how the Israelites slaughtered a lamb to ward off the divine killing of the firstborn, and ate unleavened bread because they were forced to leave in a hurry before the dough could rise; Weeks commemorates the making of the Sinai covenant fifty days after the Exodus; and Booths commemorates how the Israelites lived in temporary housing on their journey to the Promised Land.[11]

According to the book of Exodus, Passover is to be celebrated on the fourteenth day of the first month;[12] this indicates a new year beginning in the spring. The Day of Atonement (Yom Kippur) is to be observed in the seventh month—that is, in the fall.[13] But a later Jewish holy day, Rosh Hashanah (literally, "the head [i.e., beginning] of the year"), is loosely based on other passages that seem to refer to a fall new year, and is celebrated shortly before the Day of Atonement.[14]

Like the festivals of Weeks and Booths, Passover was originally a pilgrimage festival to a centrally located tribal sacred place. When there was a Temple in Jerusalem, the principal celebration of Passover was frequently there; the Passover lambs would be ritually slaughtered in the Temple and then eaten at home during the Passover meal, as the book of Exodus (12:43-46) prescribes and as is done by kosher methods in Judaism today.

Two major holy days are not found in the Torah. Purim ("lots") is linked with the story of Esther, in the book named for her. Tisha B'Av ("the ninth [day] of [the month of] Av") commemorates the destruction of the First Temple by the Babylonians in 586 BCE and of the Second Temple by the Romans in 70 CE.[15]

The only important Jewish holy day not directly or indirectly linked with the canonical Hebrew Bible is Hanukkah ("Dedication"), commemorating the rededication of the Second Temple in Jerusalem by the Maccabees in 165 BCE.[16] Lesser biblical holy days, such as the festival of the new moon, also continue to be observed by some Jews.

Which Christian holy days are based on the Bible?

Harmonization of the four Gospel accounts of the life of Jesus provides most of them, both directly and indirectly. Although the date of the birth of Jesus is not given in the Gospels, by the third century CE the Roman festival of Sol Invictus ("the unconquered Sun") was celebrated on December 25, just after the winter solstice as the days began to lengthen, and by the fourth century Christians had chosen the same date to celebrate the birth of Jesus to compete with the Roman festival. The circumcision of Jesus on the eighth day after his birth, following biblical law, comes next, coinciding with New Year's Day; the festival of the Epiphany, commemorating the visit of the "wise men from the East" (Matthew 2:1), follows on January 6.[17]

Most of the other holy days are connected with events at the end of Jesus's life and have variable dates, because they are originally based on Passover, whose date was determined by a lunar calendar.[18] These include Palm Sunday, Maundy Thursday, Good Friday, and Easter Sunday. Other holy days are calculated from Easter, including the ascension of Jesus into heaven forty days after Easter, and Pentecost, fifty days after Easter.[19]

How is Sabbath observance based on the Bible?

According to the Decalogue, the seventh day (that is, Saturday) was a day of rest, on which no work was to be performed; the word "Sabbath" is derived from the Hebrew verb *shabat*, "to cease, to rest."[20] Work is not defined, but elsewhere in the

Hebrew Bible examples in narratives, laws, and the prophets expand on this prohibition. Commercial activity was banned;[21] heavy loads were not to be carried;[22] and a fire was not to be kindled nor was one to cook.[23] Violating the Sabbath rest was a capital offense.[24] In ancient Israel, the Sabbath was also the holiest day of the week, when special sacrifices were offered and other religious services including readings, sermons, and prayers took place.

As Judaism developed, further elaborations of "work" were formulated, and debates ensued about how strict Sabbath observance was to be.[25] In the time of the Maccabees, some Jewish rebels refused to defend themselves when they were attacked on the Sabbath, but their leader Mattathias subsequently said that self-defense on the Sabbath was essential.[26] We find echoes of those debates in the Gospels, as well as in rabbinic literature.

Although the earliest Christians were Jewish and observed the Sabbath, as Christianity began to separate itself from its Jewish matrix, Christians started to observe Sunday, "the Lord's day" (Revelation 1:10),[27] as the day of worship and rest.[28] They did so to commemorate Jesus having been raised from the dead "on the first day of the week" (Mark 16:2), and also to differentiate their practice from that of Jews, just as later, Muslims will observe Friday as their day of rest, to differentiate themselves from both Jews and Christians. At various periods in Christian history, work, travel, commercial transactions, and recreation have been prohibited on the day of rest.

Some Christian groups, such as Seventh-day Adventists, correctly recognizing that there is no divine command to change the day of rest from Saturday to Sunday, have reverted to the ancient Israelite observance.

What rituals are based on the Bible?

Many religious ceremonies found in the Bible continue to be practiced both actually and symbolically in biblically based religions. For example, circumcision is practiced by both Jews and Muslims, because both groups view themselves as descended from Abraham, to whom the command to circumcise all males was first given.[29] Many Christians also practice circumcision, although more for cultural than religious reasons. In Jewish tradition, attached to the entryways in homes is often a small container called a mezuzah, inside which is a small scroll. On the scroll are written verses from Deuteronomy, beginning with the Shema ("Hear, O Israel," 6:4), which goes on to command that these words be written "on the doorposts (Hebrew *mezuzot*) of your house" (6:9). Jewish dietary laws and purification rituals are also biblically based, as are many other aspects of daily life practiced by observant Jews. The Christian rituals known as "sacraments" also have a biblical origin, especially baptism and the Eucharist or holy communion, both based on instructions of Jesus.[30]

What later religious movements are based on the Bible?

In addition to its foundational role in Judaism and Christianity, the Bible also had a profound influence on Islam. The Qur'an mentions, often in detail, the major characters of the Bible, including Abraham, Isaac, Ishmael, Jacob, Moses, David, Solomon, Job, John the Baptist, Mary the mother of Jesus, and Jesus himself.

Nineteenth-century American religious movements with their own spin on the Bible include the Church of Jesus Christ of Latter-day Saints (Mormonism), Seventh-day Adventism, Jehovah's Witnesses, and Christian Science.

How has the Bible been used in politics?

Often to provide supposed divine sanction for assumption and exercise of power. If leaders can get their subjects to believe that they have been divinely appointed, then that undercuts revolt and insurrection. Such claims begin in the Bible itself: According to some biblical sources, the first kings of Israel,

Saul and David, were designated kings of Israel by Yahweh himself. The prophet Nathan was reportedly instructed to tell David in Yahweh's name:

> I took you from the pasture, from following the sheep to be prince over my people Israel. . . . When your days are fulfilled and you lie down with your ancestors, I will raise up your offspring after you, who shall come forth from your body, and I will establish his kingdom. . . . Your house and your kingdom shall be made sure forever before me; your throne shall be established forever. (2 Samuel 7:8, 12, 16, NRSV)

Many biblical writers echo this idea of what came to be called "the divine right of kings."[31] One of the most often quoted is Paul, who advises Christians in Rome:

> Let every person be subject to the governing authorities; for there is no authority except from God, and those authorities that exist have been instituted by God. Therefore, whoever resists authority resists what God has appointed. (Romans 13:1–2, NRSV)

Such claims are found elsewhere in the ancient world, and throughout history ever since. Especially in the West, Christian rulers such as Charlemagne, Henry VIII, and Napoleon have asserted that they were divinely chosen. But Paul's words, addressed to a specific audience in a specific historical context, have often been ignored (think of the American and French revolutions against governing authorities!), as well as misused, to legitimize slavery in the United States, apartheid in South Africa, and Nazism in Germany. Moreover, disobedience to government authority is also frequently praised in the Bible. The Hebrew midwives in Egypt, Daniel and his companions in Babylon, and the observant Jews of the Maccabean revolt are notable examples.

Like many other ancient groups, the Israelites thought of themselves as a people specially chosen by their god. Later groups appropriated that status for themselves, including some Christians, some Americans, and some Israelis, often with pernicious consequences for those deemed not chosen. But the biblical basis for such claims is questionable, because different writers in different periods disagree about who specifically is chosen, and because the Bible reflects what the biblical writers thought, not what God decreed.

The Bible has also influenced ecclesiastical politics. According to the Gospel of Matthew, after Peter has identified Jesus as "the Messiah, the Son of the living God," Jesus says to him:

> You are Peter, and upon this rock I will build my church, and the gates of the netherworld shall not prevail against it. I will give you the keys to the kingdom of heaven. Whatever you bind on earth shall be bound in heaven, and whatever you loose on earth shall be loosed in heaven. (16:16, 18–19, NABRE)

In the Roman Catholic Church, this passage is understood to explain "the primacy of Peter" and his successors, the popes. But Jesus uses the same language when speaking to his disciples in Matthew 18:18,[32] so taking both texts together, other Christian denominations argue that the same authority is bestowed on all of Jesus's followers, or at least on all of the Twelve, so that no single leader has supreme authority. In any case, neither passage speaks of the transfer of authority from one generation to the next. We should also note that Paul claimed that he had equal status with Peter, nor did he hesitate to call Peter out for hypocrisy.[33]

How has the Bible influenced jurisprudence?

Much as the Qur'an has been the foundation for legal traditions in majority-Muslim countries, so too in majority-Christian countries and in the modern state of Israel, the Bible has been the basis for legal norms and practices, both implicitly and often explicitly. For example, Sabbath observance, capital punishment, lending money, and other civil and criminal matters have often been based on biblical law and teaching.

Why do people swear on the Bible?

One example of the use of the Bible in legal contexts is that oaths are often taken with one's hand on the Bible: the "swearing in" of officeholders, witnesses in court, and the like. With its direct roots in biblical law, and its background in widespread ancient judicial practice, an oath is a kind of self-curse, in which oath-takers call down divine punishment if what they swear to is not true. The raising of the right hand when swearing is probably based on biblical models.[34]

In the United States, non-Jews and non-Christians are not required to swear on the Bible, nor are Christians such as Quakers, who follow Jesus's words in the Sermon on the Mount literally: "Do not swear at all; not by heaven . . . nor by the earth . . . nor by Jerusalem. . . . Let your 'Yes' mean 'Yes' and your 'No' mean 'No'" (Matthew 5:34–37, NABRE).[35]

Sometimes oaths are accompanied by ritual ceremonies and by symbolic gestures. In Genesis, a patriarch instructs someone to swear after putting his hand on the patriarch's "thigh."[36] "Thigh" is a euphemism for the male genitals,[37] and this partially explains why "testicles" and "testimony" are related words.

How else has the Bible been used in ordinary life?

In several ways. One example is the family Bible, in which over many generations such major events as births, marriages, and deaths were written down in a special Bible kept in the home. Another is the superstitious practice of seeking advice from the Bible by opening its pages at random, and without looking putting one's finger on (or sticking a pin in) a verse, which would then supposedly predict the future or offer guidance on a course of action. This practice (called "sortes," originally meaning "lots") is known from classical antiquity using such authors as Homer and Virgil, and also in Islam using the Qur'an.

How has the Bible influenced scientific understanding?

Profoundly, at least until the Renaissance, when Copernicus and Galileo proved that biblical cosmology was simply wrong. As advances in sciences such as geology, evolutionary biology, and astrophysics continued, it became clear that biblical chronology for the age of the world was also wrong, as were its creation accounts. Such advances were a major contributing factor to the development of historical criticism, as well as to diminishing the Bible's authority.

Astonishingly, despite all the scientific evidence, Gallup surveys over the last several decades consistently report that almost half of Americans do not believe in the evolution of the human species, but rather that God created us in our present form.[38]

How has the Bible influenced the practice of medicine?

Like others in the ancient world, biblical writers often viewed disease as having a divine origin. The cure for disease was to confess one's guilt and ask for divine forgiveness. One consequence of this belief was that those closely connected to the world of the divine, such as priests and prophets, were often also what we would call medical practitioners. The prophets Elisha and Isaiah are both described as healers, as also is Jesus.[39] Priests were involved with both diagnosis and treatment, especially for skin disorders (which most translations call "leprosy").[40] Healings were therefore considered miraculous, because of divine action; Sirach asserts that physicians' "gift of healing comes from the Most High" (38:2).[41]

It is often difficult to provide modern diagnoses for diseases described in the Bible. The Gospel of Mark recounts how Jesus healed a boy who is described as being possessed by "a spirit that makes him unable to speak; and whenever it seizes him, it dashes him down; and he foams and grinds his teeth and becomes rigid" (9:17–18, NRSV). But in Matthew's version of this healing, the boy is described as being "moonstruck,"[42] and often falling into fire and water (17:15); again, demonic possession is the ultimate cause.

Such beliefs were pervasive until the development of modern medicine, and vestiges still exist in modern culture. Physical and especially mental illnesses are sometimes attributed to moral failings, and even sometimes to Satan. Healing ministries are still practiced in many religious groups, and the Roman Catholic Church still requires two miraculous cures (attested by persons other than the ones who are healed) for a person to be made a saint.

8

BIBLICAL CONCEPTS

What do I mean by "biblical concepts"?

By biblical concepts I mean major ideas and themes that are often grouped under the rubric "biblical theology." It is a mistake, I think, to speak of "*the* theology" of the Bible, or of the Hebrew Bible, or of the Old Testament, or of the New Testament, as though across or within the various canons there is a single viewpoint; rather, it is better to think of the theology of Jeremiah or the theology of Paul, and so forth. In this chapter I have had to be selective, and am providing only a sample of biblical concepts. The chapter will also further illustrate the interpretive strategies already discussed.

Many tomes have been written on the concepts I treat here, and on many others. Readers can learn of these by looking at the biblical dictionaries and encyclopedias listed on page 177 in the General section of Further Reading, and especially *The Oxford Encyclopedia of the Bible and Theology*, edited by Samuel L. Balentine (2 volumes; New York: Oxford University Press, 2015).

Who is Yahweh?

Yahweh is the personal name of the god of Israel, used nearly seven thousand times in the Hebrew Bible. Although according to one Pentateuchal source (see page 87), this name began to be used in primeval times,[1] according to others, it was first revealed to Moses.[2] Its meaning is disputed, but it seems to be an abbreviated sentence name meaning something like "he brings into being."[3] Because by the late biblical period the name had become considered too sacred to pronounce, the vocalization in the Masoretic Text indicates that when it occurs in the Hebrew Bible it should be read as "Adonay," "My Lord."[4] In the Septuagint Yahweh is consistently translated "Lord" (Greek *kyrios*), and most subsequent translations have also used this pious substitution, usually with small caps: "Lord." The name is also frequently referred to as the Tetragrammaton ("the four letters" YHWH). Another pious substitution for Yahweh is simply "the Name."

What other names and titles does Yahweh have?

The second most frequent title used for the god of Israel is *Elohim*, derived from the common Semitic word for "god" (also found, for example, in Arabic *Allah*). It is masculine plural in form, and is often used in Hebrew in this sense to refer to other deities. But although grammatically plural, it is also used in a singular sense of the god of Israel, and usually translated "God," as in the frequent affirmation "Yahweh is God."[5]

The title "Lord of Hosts"[6] designates Yahweh as the leader (and possibly the creator) of the heavenly armies, "the host of heaven" (see, for example, 1 Kings 22:19; compare also Joshua 5:14). Another frequent designation of Yahweh is as a king. He is also described metaphorically as a father and sometimes as a mother, as a husband, a rock, and so forth.

How did monotheism develop?

Monotheism, the belief that there is only one god, developed in ancient Israel and became a distinctive feature of Judaism and its derived religions Christianity and Islam. Other ancient and many later religions had systems in which there were multiple gods, each often representing an aspect of nature, such as the sun, moon, and stars, the seas and rivers, thunder and rain, trees, and grain. The world of the gods was hierarchical: The assembly of the gods was presided over by a divine ruler, often the chief deity of a city or region.

We find many traces of this mythology in the Bible. Yahweh is frequently acclaimed as the most powerful of the gods.[7] He presides over the divine assembly, often addressing its members in the plural.[8] These lesser divine beings are sometimes called the "sons of God," which many translations soften to "heavenly beings," "angels," or the like.[9]

According to the First Commandment (Exodus 20:3), however, although these other deities exist, only Yahweh is to be worshipped. That at least was the ideal, but seldom the reality, as frequent biblical prohibitions and condemnations of the worship of other deities make clear. The deities whom the ancient Israelites worshipped included, unsurprisingly, those of their neighbors: Astarte, the main goddess of Sidon; Chemosh, the chief deity of Moab; Milcom, the chief deity of the Ammonites; the Canaanite god Baal and the goddess Asherah; the Mesopotamian dying and rising god Tammuz; and the sun, the moon, and the stars, to name just some.[10]

The process by which this literary and popular polytheism became strict monotheism is not entirely clear. It was certainly complete by the sixth century BCE, when an anonymous prophet, speaking in Yahweh's name, proclaimed: "I am God, and there is no other" (Isaiah 45:22, New Revised Standard Version [NRSV]).[11] Significantly, we find anticipations of this in other prophetic material. A legend about the ninth-century BCE prophet Elijah (whose name means "My god is Yah[weh]") describes how in a contest with the prophets of Baal, he alone was able to call down fire from heaven, with the result that the people proclaimed: "The LORD indeed is God; the LORD indeed is God" (1 Kings 18:39, NRSV). I suspect that the move toward monotheism developed in prophetic circles as a reaction to the growing foreign control and eventual destruction of both the northern kingdom of Israel and the southern kingdom of Judah. Typically in the ancient world, if a city or country was defeated, that meant that the god or gods of the victors were more powerful than those of the losers. But the Israelites' frequent defeats would have caused a kind of cognitive dissonance for believers that Yahweh was the most powerful of the gods, so the belief that Yahweh was just Israel's god broadened to the belief that Yahweh was the god of the whole world, the lord of history as it were. Isaiah has Yahweh claim that powerful Assyria was simply a weapon in his hands for punishing the Israelites for their idolatry and social injustice.[12] The logical conclusion of this development was strict monotheism.

With the development of strict monotheism, the divine members of Yahweh's court were demoted, some to angels and some to devils (especially Satan), and Jewish thinkers invented elaborate systems of angelology and demonology, adopted and expanded by Christians and Muslims.

What did early Christians mean when they called Jesus "son of God"?

Jesus of Nazareth was an actual person who lived in the early first century CE. Different New Testament writers have different understandings of what else he was. The most central, and in some ways the most difficult for Christian theology because it seems inconsistent with monotheism, is that he was the "son of God."

The Gospel of Mark starts with these words: "The beginning of the good news about Jesus Christ, the son of God" (NRSV). But what meanings did Mark and other New Testament writers think that the title had?

In some Jewish scriptures, a righteous person can be called God's son.[13] We know that this was in the mind of some early Christian writers because of the different versions of the words of the Roman military official in charge of Jesus's execution. In

Mark, followed by Matthew, he says: "Truly this man was a son of God" (Mark 15:39; Matthew 27:54, my translation), but in Luke he says: "Certainly this was a righteous man" (that is, "innocent"— see further page 132; Luke 23:47, King James Version [KJV]).

Israel is also understood metaphorically to be God's son. In his infancy narrative, Matthew presents Jesus as a new Israel, who like the Israel of old went down to Egypt and then returned to the Promised Land; Matthew makes this explicit by saying "This was to fulfill what had been spoken by the Lord through the prophet, 'Out of Egypt I have called my son'" (2:15, quoting Hosea 11.1).[14]

Furthermore, the concept of "son of God" is also used in the Hebrew Bible to refer to the reigning king in Jerusalem in David's line. The prophet Nathan, speaking in Yahweh's name, says of David's successor, "I will be a father to him, and he will be a son to me" (2 Samuel 7:14, Common English Bible [CEB]), a verse quoted with reference to Jesus in Hebrews 1:5. Part of the coronation ceremony of Israelite kings included a kind of symbolic adoption of the king by Yahweh, as in Psalm 2, where Yahweh announces, "You are my son; today I have become your father" (v. 7, CEB).[15] In the Roman Empire in which the biblical writers lived, "son of god" (Latin *divi filius*) was also a title of the reigning emperor, appearing on coins of Augustus and many of his successors.

Yet another meaning is provided by Jesus himself. He is quoted as addressing God with the Aramaic word *abba*, which means "father."[16] But this does not necessarily mean that he thought of himself as having a special relationship to God; after all, he taught his disciples when they prayed to address God as "Father";[17] probably echoing Jesus's teaching, Paul says: "God has sent the spirit of his son into our hearts, crying 'Abba! Father!'" (Galatians 4:6; see also Romans 8:15).

Whatever Jesus himself may have thought, it is clear that some New Testament writers thought that his relationship to God was unique. In their infancy narratives, Matthew and

Luke both report that Mary was a virgin and became pregnant by direct divine action. The idea that gods can impregnate human women is found in the Bible[18] and is a common motif of classical mythology, so it would not have seemed as extraordinary to a first-century audience as it does to us. Still, the belief in the "Virgin Birth" took hold and became a core element in Christian understanding of Jesus as son of God. In the New Testament, this understanding in its fullest sense is found in the Gospel of John, which repeatedly speaks of Jesus's unique relationship with God, as when he reportedly says, "The father and I are one" (10:30).[19]

Another way of examining the overlapping meanings of the title "son of God" is to look at New Testament sources in roughly chronological order. The earliest source is Paul. In his letter to the Romans, written about 60 CE, he describes himself as an apostle of "the gospel of God . . . concerning his son, who was descended from David according to the flesh, and was declared to be son of God with power according to the spirit of holiness by resurrection from the dead, Jesus Christ our Lord" (1:1–4, NRSV). For Paul, then, Jesus became God's son when he was raised from the dead. The earliest Gospel, Mark, probably written shortly after 70, has Jesus's divine sonship take place at the beginning of his ministry, when he was baptized by John and a voice from heaven proclaimed "You are my son, the beloved" (1:11, NRSV), a kind of adoption as it were. The Gospels of Matthew and Luke, probably written in the 80s, both, although in very different narratives, say that Mary, Jesus's mother, was a virgin and therefore Jesus was God's son in an almost biological sense. Finally, the latest Gospel, John, which like Mark has no infancy narrative, describes Jesus in its opening verses as the eternally existing word of God, his only son, who at a particular historical moment "became flesh and made his home among us" (1:14, CEB). We thus see both diversity and development in early Christian understanding of Jesus as son of God.

What does "son of man" mean?

Another title used of Jesus is "son of man," which also has several meanings. In the Hebrew Bible it means "human being" or "mortal," which is how the NRSV translates it, using inclusive language, when the prophet Ezekiel is addressed.[20] The distribution of the phrase "son of man" in the New Testament is significant. It occurs dozens of times, almost exclusively in the Gospels and almost always in speeches by Jesus.[21] One widely accepted interpretation is that "son of man" was a phrase characteristically used by Jesus to refer to himself, as in Jesus's saying "Foxes have holes and birds of the air have nests, but the son of man has nowhere to lay his head" (Matthew 8:20 = Luke 9:58).

A third meaning of "son of man" is derived from the book of Daniel. In an apocalyptic dream, Daniel sees:

> one like a son of man coming, with the clouds of heaven. He approached the Ancient of Days and was led into his presence; all peoples, nations and men of every language worshiped him. His dominion is an everlasting dominion that will not pass away, and his kingdom is one that will never be destroyed. (Daniel 7:13–14, New International Version])

In Jewish writings after the book of Daniel, the figure described as being human-like ("like a son of man") is increasingly identified as messianic. Many scholars identify Jesus as an apocalyptic prophet, and it is possible that he also used the term "son of man" to mean himself as God's agent in bringing about "the kingdom of God" and thus as the future ruler described in Daniel 7.[22]

What is a messiah?

The English word "messiah" comes from Hebrew *mashiach*, meaning "anointed one." In ancient Israel, as elsewhere in the ancient Near East, anointing with oil was part of an induction ceremony for those thought to have a close relationship with the divine, especially kings, priests, and prophets; anointing continues to be part of the ritual for various forms of ordination and in some coronation ceremonies.[23]

In the Hebrew Bible, the term *mashiach* is almost always used of past and present persons chosen to carry out the divine plan. So, Saul, the first king of Israel, is called "the anointed of Yahweh" by David both before and after Saul's death.[24] Only when the monarchy had ceased to exist is the word used of one or more future rulers, usually understood to be descendants of David.[25]

There thus developed in Judaism the expectation that God would be true to his promises that David's kingdom would endure forever, and by restoring Davidic kingship to Israel would deliver it from foreign rule.[26] In the New Testament, Jesus is identified as this longed-for anointed one, the Messiah; his Greek title *christos* is simply a translation of the Hebrew term.

But although the sign on Jesus's cross said "King of the Jews," he was crucified. In order to reconcile his apparent failure to do what a messiah was supposed to do, early Christians came to believe that Jesus would return to complete his mission at some time in the future.

When will the Messiah come?

Many early Christians thought that Jesus would return very soon. Writing to the Corinthian church, Paul says that "the time is running out" (1 Corinthians 7:29) and that "the world in its present form is passing away" (7:31), for "the end of the ages has come" (10:11, all New American Bible, Revised Edition). One early Christian prayer was the Aramaic petition *"Marana tha"* ("Our Lord, come," 1 Corinthians 16:22).[27] Jesus himself is quoted as saying, "There are some standing here who will not taste death before they see the son of man coming in his kingdom" (Matthew 16:28).[28]

As time went on and Jesus did not return, some began to doubt that he ever would.[29] But both many Jews and many Christians believe that the Messiah will eventually come; as the Nicene Creed puts it, speaking of Jesus: "He will come again to judge the living and the dead." Over the centuries, many individuals have claimed to be or been identified as the Messiah, but none of the assertions that the end time is near have yet been fulfilled.

What significance does the title "son of David" have?

Another messianic title applied to Jesus is "son of David," because of the divine promise that David's descendants would rule from Jerusalem forever.[30] Its messianic significance is clear when we compare the crowd's acclamation in different Gospels as Jesus enters Jerusalem in the week before his death: "Hosanna to the son of David!" (Matthew 21:9), and "Blessed is the king who comes in the name of the Lord" (Luke 19:38, NRSV).

The precise title "son of David" is used of Jesus only in the Synoptic Gospels, and only by persons other than Jesus himself, further suggesting that it was a popular title.[31] It is especially prominent in Matthew, where it is used more than half a dozen times, only two of which have parallels in Mark and Luke. Both Matthew and Luke in their genealogies of Jesus (Matthew 1:1–17; Luke 3:23–38) trace his ancestry back through Joseph to David, although somewhat differently.[32] Moreover, Matthew and Luke agree that Jesus was born in Bethlehem, David's ancestral home, in fulfillment of a messianic prophecy, although other New Testament texts suggest that he was born in Nazareth.[33]

What is a covenant, and which are the most important covenants?

In the Bible, a covenant is a binding agreement between two parties. The most frequent Hebrew word for covenant is *berit*, which was originally a legal term used for such matters as the settlement of boundary disputes, treaties, and marriage.[34] The term is then used by analogy for God's relationships with individuals and groups, including Noah and his descendants; Abraham and his descendants; all Israel; and David and his descendants.

In Hebrew, the verb used for covenant-making literally means "to cut," probably because the sacrifice of an animal often accompanied covenant ceremonies.[35] A synonym for *berit* is *edut*, often translated as "testament," which is derived from the Hebrew word for "witness," since contracts in antiquity, as in the present, were generally witnessed.

The covenant with Noah occurs after the Flood. God promises Noah and his sons that he will never again destroy the world by a flood, and he puts his bow, his weapon as a storm god, in the sky to remind himself of the promise.[36] Since, according to Genesis, Noah is the ancestor of all humans after the Flood, the commandment given to Noah prohibiting the taking of human life is viewed as universally binding; rabbinic tradition will expand this into seven Noahide laws.

Different sources in Genesis describe two variations of the covenant that God makes with Abraham. In one, Yahweh promises to give the land of Canaan in which Abraham is then living to Abraham's descendants.[37] In the other, he promises Abraham not only the land of Canaan, but also a multitude of descendants, and in exchange requires that from then on, Abraham and his male offspring be circumcised.[38]

Easily the most important covenant in the Bible is that between God and Israel made at Mount Sinai after the Exodus from Egypt. It is sometimes also called the "Mosaic covenant," because Moses was the intermediary between God and the Israelites. This covenant is conditional in the sense that God will reward them profusely as long as they keep its stipulations, but punish them severely if they do not. The stipulations are the many laws found in the books of Exodus through Deuteronomy, beginning with the "ten words," the Ten Commandments.[39] No other ancient Near Eastern group yet known characterized its relationship with a deity as a "covenant."

Another important covenant is that between God and David. Although there is no extended narrative describing the making of this covenant, repeated references to it make clear that it was a central component of royal self-definition and self-promotion. Most texts describe this Davidic covenant as unconditional: that is, God guarantees that even if David's successors act wrongfully, the dynasty that he founded will rule forever.[40]

What is the "new covenant"?

The phrase "new covenant," which underlies the term "New Testament," occurs only eight times in the Bible. Speaking in the name of God, the prophet Jeremiah proclaims that because the Israelites had broken the Sinai covenant, "The time is coming, declares the LORD, when I will make a new covenant with the people of Israel and Judah . . . for I will forgive their wrongdoing and never again remember their sins" (31:31, 34, CEB). For Jeremiah, this was not a brand-new covenant with a new group, but rather a renewal of the original Sinai covenant, with the same participants: God and the Israelites.

Some New Testament writers, however, appropriated the phrase. It is used by Luke and Paul in their accounts of the Last Supper,[41] and also by Paul in 2 Corinthians 3:6. Most significant is its use in the letter to the Hebrews, which, after quoting Jeremiah, gives this interpretation:

In speaking of "a new covenant," he has made the first one obsolete. And what is obsolete and growing old will soon disappear. (8:13, NRSV; see also 9:15; 12:24)

This is an example of what is called supersessionism, the view that Christianity has replaced Judaism, and, along with other parts of the New Testament (see further pages 154–55), has tragically contributed to Christian anti-Semitism.

What is righteousness?

Many important biblical concepts have entered theological vocabulary because of the familiarity of the KJV, although the words used by its translators do not always adequately convey the nuances of the biblical writers' views. One example is righteousness, a word occurring hundreds of times in the KJV, including nearly forty times in Paul's letter to the Romans. The Hebrew word generally translated that way (*tsedaqah*), and to some extent the Greek word used to translate it in the Septuagint and thus in the New Testament (*dikaiosune*), have the primary meanings of honesty and innocence, first in a legal sense, and, by extension, in a moral sense, especially in God's judgment.

What is theodicy?

Theodicy is a word derived from Greek that means "divine justice." Unlike the gods of other nations, who according to their mythology are often capricious and played favorites, the one God of the Bible is supposed to act justly. When Yahweh informed Abraham that he was about to destroy Sodom for some unspecified sin, Abraham challenged him by asking:

> If there are fifty innocent people in the city, will you destroy the whole city? . . . Surely you won't kill the innocent with the guilty. . . . The judge of all the earth has to act justly. (Genesis 18:24–25, Good News Bible)

The biblical God, at least in theory, is one who rewards the innocent, the righteous, and punishes the guilty.

Why "at least in theory"? Because another attribute of the biblical God is his mercy. An ancient hymn, quoted or alluded to more than a dozen times elsewhere in the Bible, celebrates this, and also complicates the issue:

> Yahweh, Yahweh: a compassionate and merciful god,
>   slow to anger and great in mercy and
>   trustworthiness;
> preserving mercy to a thousand generations,
>   forgiving transgression and wickedness and sin;
> but also not acquitting the guilty,
>   reckoning fathers' sins on sons and grandsons
>   to the third and fourth generations. (Exodus 34:6–7,
>   my translation)[42]

This formula suggests that divine mercy is more important than divine justice. That is a good thing: It makes no sense to pray for forgiveness to a deity who is not merciful. But the formula also creates a problem: How is it just to punish children and grandchildren for their parents' sins? The prophets Jeremiah and Ezekiel recognized this; Ezekiel says:

> The life of the parent and the life of the child belong to me. Only the one who sins will die. (18:4, CEB; see also Jeremiah 31:29–30)

But this raises yet another problem: Does God in fact always punish the wicked and reward the righteous? Obviously not, as Ecclesiastes observed:

> Look at what happens in the world: sometimes the righteous get the punishment of the wicked, and the wicked get the reward of the righteous. (8:14, Good News Bible)

The book of Job is an extended poetic examination of these questions, but provides no conclusive answers according to most interpreters. God's frequent failure to reward the righteous and to punish the wicked while they are alive is one factor in the development of belief in an afterlife.

What were biblical writers' views about life after death?

Complicated. One biblical Hebrew euphemism for dying that that one is "gathered to one's people." That implies some postmortem existence, as also does the presence of food offerings in tombs in ancient Israel and elsewhere.[43] A vivid example of belief in some kind of personal immortality is the account of the medium who, at King Saul's request, summoned the spirit of the dead prophet Samuel from the underworld. Although such activity, called necromancy, was prohibited in biblical law,[44] perhaps because it competed with priestly and prophetic authority, it apparently worked: When Saul asked the medium what she saw, she replied, "I see a god rising from the earth" (1 Samuel 28:13, New American Bible, Revised Edition).[45] This suggests that in some Israelite circles, as often elsewhere in the ancient world, at least some of the dead were deified.

With the exception of Enoch and Elijah, who were taken up to heaven,[46] for the Israelites the dead resided in the underworld, called "Sheol."[47] This is where everyone went—the powerful and the weak, the righteous and the wicked—and for most, if not all, there was no return.[48] Like the grave, Sheol was a dank, dirty place, and for some writers, such existence as the dead had was greatly diminished. As one of the psalmists, praying to God not to let him die, said: "In Sheol who can give you praise?" (Psalm 6:5).[49] Sheol thus resembled Hades in Greek mythology, which is how Sheol is translated in the Septuagint; the same Greek term is also used in the New Testament.

But there were also dissenters, one of the most prominent of whom is Ecclesiastes. Not only did he argue that there was no pattern of divine rewards and punishments in this life, but, he thought, death was final:

> The living know that they will die. But the dead know nothing at all. There is no more reward for them; even the memory of them is lost. . . . For there is no work or thought or wisdom in Sheol. (9:5, CEB; 9:10, NRSV)

By the Hellenistic period, however, different views began to emerge, based in part on a dualistic understanding of the human person. In Greek thought, persons had not just a body but also a soul (Greek *psyche*), which survived death. Some biblical writers adopted the idea that either at death or at some time in the future the souls of the righteous would enjoy a glorious afterlife.[50] Thus, even though they may have died a terrible death at the hands of the wicked, "the souls of the righteous are in the hand of God," and eventually

> They will shine forth and will run like sparks through the stubble. They will govern nations and rule over peoples. (Wisdom 3:1, 7–8)

A logical consequence of the eventual reward of the righteous is that of the eventual punishment of the wicked, which also developed in the late biblical period. Theologically at least, these beliefs partially solve the dilemma of theodicy: In the end, God will indeed be just. In Jewish and Christian thought, elaborate mythologies developed about the afterlife, with often vivid descriptions of heaven and hell. Some Jews, and many Christians, still accept the substance of these descriptions, although modern astronomy and geology make the premodern locations of heaven and hell impossible.

In some circles, belief not just about the soul's immortality but about bodily resurrection also developed. The only clear example in the Hebrew Bible is in a revelation by the angel Gabriel to Daniel:

> Many of those who sleep in the dust of the earth shall awake, some to everlasting life and some to shame and contempt. Those who are wise shall shine like the brightness of the sky, and those who lead many to righteousness, like the stars forever and ever. (Daniel 12:2–3, NRSV)

In Judaism, bodily resurrection was still being debated in the first century CE, as both the Gospels and Josephus make clear.[51] But, influenced by the belief that God had raised Jesus from the dead, bodily resurrection is a view found in most New Testament writers.

What did early Christians believe about Jesus's resurrection?

The earliest evidence for Christian belief in Jesus's resurrection is in Paul's first letter to the Corinthians. Paul summarizes the oral traditions that he had heard: On the third day after Jesus's crucifixion (that is, Sunday, which becomes the Christian Easter), Jesus was raised from the dead "in accordance with the scriptures"; then he appeared to Cephas (Peter), to the Twelve, to "more than five hundred brothers," to James, then to all the apostles. "Last of all," Paul says, "he appeared to me" (1 Corinthians 15:3–8).

We find accounts of these appearances elsewhere in the New Testament. Let us begin with Paul himself. In his account of his call to preach to non-Jews, Paul speaks of God "revealing" Jesus to him, but gives no details about that revelation (Galatians 1:16). Three later accounts of Paul's call in Acts of Apostles do provide more details, but they are not entirely consistent with each other.[52] All feature a bright light and a dis-embodied voice that says, "I am Jesus."

The four Gospels, and Acts 1, report appearances by Jesus, preceded by the discovery of his empty tomb by one or more women. Matthew and John further report that Jesus appeared to one or more of the women before he appeared to his male followers. But these Gospel accounts correspond only loosely to those listed by Paul, and Paul mentions neither the empty tomb nor the women who discovered it, nor Jesus's appear-ances to women.

The appearances are notable in several ways. For one thing, Jesus comes and goes something like a ghost.[53] For another, his followers often initially fail to recognize him, perhaps because, as Paul puts it, their experience was not of Jesus's physical body but of his "spiritual body" (1 Corinthians 15:44). What is clear from these diverse accounts is that the early Christians believed that the Jesus whom they had known during his life continued to be present to them somehow. They expressed that belief in vivid, if different, accounts of Jesus appearing to them.

Eventually, the appearances stopped, with Jesus being taken up into heaven. Writing several decades after Jesus's death, the Gospel writers seem to have wanted to assure their own audiences and subsequent generations of Christians that Jesus could continue to be present to them, even if he were no longer appearing. Significantly, Mark's Gospel has no appear-ances of the risen Jesus; as Jesus reportedly tells the doubting Thomas, "Blessed are those who have not seen, and yet have come to believe" (John 20:29, NRSV).

Does the Bible have a central theme?

There is more than one possible answer to this question, but I think a case can be made that the Israelites' Exodus from Egypt under Moses's leadership is certainly one central theme. According to many biblical writers, it was the defining event in Israel's history, in which a group of runaway slaves became a people, in fact, the people of God.

So important is the Exodus event that it almost gives the Bible its shape. In the Hebrew Bible, the Exodus is alluded to near the beginning of Genesis,[54] and the very last words of the Tanakh in the Jewish canon, referring to the return of Babylonian exiles to Jerusalem, have a kind of Exodus flavor: "Let him go up" (2 Chronicles 36:23).[55] Throughout the Jewish scriptures, in prose and poetry, in prophecy and psalms, the Exodus is celebrated and recalled. "Remember that you were a slave in the land of Egypt," the book of Deuteronomy urges frequently,[56] and "remember" is what the Israelites and subsequently the Jewish people have done. The reenactment of the Exodus in the annual celebration of Passover has continued for more than three thousand years.

The Exodus also serves as a model for subsequent events in biblical and later history. For example, Second Isaiah especially interprets the return from Babylon as a new Exodus, and, in modern times, the migration of Jews from all over the world to the ancient Promised Land of Canaan has been viewed by many of them as another Exodus.

Not surprisingly, given its Jewish origins, the New Testament is also steeped in Exodus allusions. In the Gospel of Matthew, Jesus is presented as a new Israel who goes down to Egypt and returns from it to the Promised Land. He is also a new Moses, rescued as an infant from a murderous ruler, and, later, expounding his teaching in five great sermons—recalling the five books of Moses—the first of which is the Sermon on the Mount, recalling Mount Sinai. In Luke's account of Jesus's transfiguration, he appears in glory alongside Moses and the prophet Elijah, who are speaking with him of his "exodus" that he is about to accomplish in Jerusalem—his death and resurrection.[57] In the Synoptic Gospels, Jesus's last supper is a Passover seder, and in John he is the Passover lamb who takes away the sin of the world.[58]

In Christian ritual, baptism is described as a new Exodus, an escape from slavery to sin by a passage through water. Exodus language is also used in later contexts—for example, in writings of the Puritan colonizers of New England, who saw themselves as God's new Israel, escaping oppression and crossing a body of water en route to a new Canaan.

9

BIBLICAL VALUES

What are the Bible's highest values?

When the early first-century CE rabbi Hillel was asked by a prospective convert to explain the whole Torah while the prospective convert was standing on one foot, Hillel reportedly replied: "What is hateful to you, do not do to your fellow. That is the whole Torah, and the rest is commentary" (b. Shabbat 31a).[1] Hillel's near contemporary, Jesus, the rabbi from Nazareth, is said to have put it this way: "Do to others whatever you would have them do to you. This is the law and the prophets" (Matthew 7:12, New American Bible, Revised Edition [NABRE]).[2]

These parallel statements of the essence of biblical tradition are elaborated throughout the Jewish and Christian scriptures. The Ten Commandments prohibit any detrimental actions toward one's neighbor, and Leviticus 19:18 has this positive command: "Love your neighbor as yourself" (New International Version [NIV]). Love of neighbor is repeatedly promoted as one of the most important laws in the Bible. When he was asked which commandment in the Torah was the greatest, Jesus is recorded as replying:

You shall love the Lord your God with all your heart, and with all your soul, and with all your mind. This is the great and first commandment. And a second is like it, You shall love your neighbor as yourself. On these two commandments depend all the law and the prophets. (Matthew 22:37–40, Revised Standard Version)[3]

Other ancient Jewish thinkers agreed; here are two examples. According to Paul, ""The whole law is summed up in a single commandment, 'You shall love your neighbor as yourself'" (Galatians 5:14, New Revised Standard Version [NRSV]).[4] Rabbi Akiva (late first/early second century) said much the same: "'Love your neighbor as yourself' is the greatest principle in the Torah" (Sifra Qedoshim 4.12).[5]

Who is a neighbor?

Given the Bible's many authors and long history of composition, it is not surprising that we find more than one meaning. In the narrowest sense, a neighbor is someone living nearby. More broadly, in ancient Israelite law a neighbor is often a fellow Israelite, to whom one had special obligations, which the Ten Commandments specify.[6]

But the love command is not restricted to one's neighbor. Perhaps a better way to approach the question is to ask which persons the biblical writers command one to love. So, we also find the command: "The alien who resides with you shall be as the citizen among you; you shall love the alien as yourself" (Leviticus 19:34, NRSV);[7] it was not just fellow Israelites, then, whom an Israelite was to love, but non-Israelites as well, especially "resident aliens," often better translated as "immigrants."[8] Moreover, the Israelites are to recall their own experience as resident aliens in Egypt, and thus implicitly to imitate God, "who loves the resident alien" (Deuteronomy 10:18, my translation).

And not just friends, but also foes: Jesus said, "Love your enemies" (Matthew 5:44; Luke 6:22, 35),[9] and, like love of neighbor, this was not an entirely new idea of Jesus. A law in Deuteronomy concerns lost animals:

> If you see your brother's ox or sheep straying, do not ignore it, but take it back to him. . . . Do the same if you find your brother's donkey or his cloak or anything that he loses. Do not ignore it. If you see your brother's donkey or his ox fallen on the road, do not ignore it. Help him get it to its feet. (Deuteronomy 22:1–4, NIV)

But a variant (and probably earlier version) of this law in Exodus states:

> If you come across your enemy's ox or donkey wandering off, be sure to take it back to him. If you see the donkey of someone who hates you fallen down under its load, do not leave it there: be sure you help him with it. (Exodus 23:4–5, NIV)

Jesus's statement thus has biblical precedent, which extends the command to love without limit.[10]

Also noteworthy is that the expansion of Jesus's command to love one's enemies in Matthew compares it to divine action:

> Your father in heaven . . . makes his sun rise on the evil and on the good, and sends rain on the righteous and the unrighteous on the just and the unjust. . . . Be perfect, therefore, as your heavenly father is perfect. (Matthew 5:45, 48, NRSV)

How else can one show love for one's neighbor?

In addition to helping a neighbor with his fallen beast of burden (animal rights activists take note!), biblical writers repeatedly emphasize concern for the most vulnerable in society: immigrants, and the poor, and widows and orphans, who in a patriarchal society had no male protectors. That concern is not just abstract:

> Whenever you are reaping the harvest of your field and you leave some grain in the field, don't go back and get it. Let it go to the immigrants, the orphans, and the widows so that the LORD your God blesses you in all that you do. Similarly, when you beat the olives of your olive trees, don't go back over them twice. Let the leftovers go to the immigrants, the orphans, and the widows. Again, when you pick the grapes of your vineyard, don't pick them over twice. Let the leftovers go to the immigrants, the orphans, and the widows. (Deuteronomy 24:19–21, Common English Bible [CEB])[11]

Drawing on Matthew 25:31–46, Thomas Aquinas catalogued the particulars of loving one's neighbor under the seven "corporal works of mercy": feeding the hungry, giving drink to the thirsty, clothing the naked, welcoming the guest-stranger, visiting the sick, ransoming the captive, and burying the dead.[12] Matthew himself draws on earlier biblical material; a passage in the book of Isaiah anticipates the views of Hillel, Jesus, and Akiva:

> Is not this the fast that I choose:
> > to loose the bonds of injustice,
> > to undo the thongs of the yoke.
> to let the oppressed go free,
> > and to break every yoke?
> Is it not to share your bread with the hungry,
> > and bring the homeless poor into your house;
> when you see the naked, to cover them,
> > and not hiding from your own kin?
> > > (Isaiah 58:6–7, NRSV)[13]

Is the command to love one's neighbor consistently observed in the Bible?

Unfortunately not, but given the Bible's long and complicated literary history this is not surprising. Even God himself is not always a model for human conduct, frequently ordering extermination not just of his enemies, but of anyone guilty of worshipping other gods or breaking other commands of his. Although he reportedly "has no favorites" (Deuteronomy 10:17, NABRE),[14] in the last plague of the Exodus from Egypt he kills the firstborn not only of Pharaoh, but of all the Egyptians, including "the firstborn of the female slave who is behind the handmill," "the firstborn of the prisoner . . . in the dungeon, and all the firstborn of the livestock" (Exodus 11:5; 12:29, NRSV) while sparing his own enslaved people. He also commands that when the Israelites get to the land of Canaan, they should kill their neighbors in the locational sense, the men, women, and children who live there, and sometimes even their livestock.[15]

We find the same violent God in the New Testament as well, especially in the book of Revelation, where "those who do not have the seal of God on their foreheads" will be almost sadistically tortured at divine instigation by monstrous locusts for five months (Revelation 9:3–10). Much of biblical history consists of war rather than peace, hatred rather than love, and that has been used throughout history to justify violence against others.

What does the Bible say about same-sex relationships?

Not very much, and what it does say is often overemphasized. The only explicit prohibitions of male same-sex relations in the Hebrew Bible are two parallel laws in Leviticus:

> Thou shalt not lie with mankind as with womankind: it is an abomination. (18:22, King James Version [KJV])

If a man also lie with mankind, as he lieth with a woman, both of them have committed an abomination: they shall surely be put to death; their blood shall be upon them. (20:13, KJV)

The Hebrew word translated "abomination" occurs well over a hundred times in the Bible.[16] It is generally used for unacceptable religious and social practices, especially idolatry, ritual impurity, and what some biblical writers considered improper sexual relationships, such as incest.[17]

Other "abominations" are no longer considered such by some faith communities. For example, for most Christians, eating pork and shellfish is acceptable, although it is prohibited and called an abomination.[18] Moreover, only fanatical literalists would insist that the death penalty should be applied to males engaging in same-sex activity. The Hebrew Bible says nothing about sexual relationships between women.

There are no unambiguous examples of same-sex relationships in biblical narrative. Some scholars have proposed that David and Jonathan were sexual partners. Certainly to our ears some descriptions of their relationship seem to use double entendre. We are told that Jonathan loved David, that he took off the robe he was wearing and gave it to David, and that at one of their last meetings before Jonathan's death, they kissed each other.[19] Moreover, in his lament for Jonathan, David says, "Your love for me was more wonderful than the love of women" (2 Samuel 1:26, my translation). Similarly, some writers have seen a sexual relationship between Jesus and the unnamed "disciple whom Jesus loved," usually identified as John, who was leaning on his chest at the Last Supper.[20] But in both examples, the language is probably better interpreted in the context of ancient patriarchal societies, in which males could have especially close relationships.

The New Testament has a bit more to say on both male and probably also female same-sex relationships. In 1 Corinthians

6:9 and 1 Timothy 1:10, "males who bed males"[21]—a phrase that echoes the prohibitions in Leviticus—are linked with murderers, perjurers, idolaters, and other types of sinners. And in his letter to the Romans, Paul elaborates on God's punishment of those who refused to acknowledge him:

> Therefore God handed them over to degrading passions. Their females exchanged natural relations for unnatural, and the males likewise gave up natural relations with females and burned with lust for one another. Males did shameful things with males and thus received in their own persons the due penalty for their perversity. (Romans 1:26–27, NABRE)

If "their females exchanged natural relations for unnatural" refers to female sexual relations with other females, paralleling the following reference to male sexual relations with other males, then this is the only explicit biblical mention of such activity. Still, some scholars have suggested that "unnatural relations" refers to oral or anal sex between females and males. If so, then the Bible has no condemnation of lesbians. It may be, however, that Paul is being deliberately ambiguous, and that both meanings are possible.

But the authors of Leviticus were writing more than 2,500 years ago, and Paul almost 2,000 years ago. Their understanding of and views about sexual orientation and gender identity were different from ours today; concepts such as "homosexuality," to say nothing of LGBTQ+, would have been incomprehensible to them. So Paul's understanding of what is "natural" was culturally conditioned; he also describes men having long hair as unnatural.[22]

Finally, it is worth noting that nowhere in the Gospels is Jesus quoted as discussing same-sex relations. For that matter, he does not say much about sexual morality in general.

What about the sin of Sodom?

The word "sodomy," meaning anal intercourse, is derived from the name of the biblical city of Sodom. But was sodomy the sin for which God punished Sodom?

In the book of Genesis, Sodom, and its sister-city Gomorrah, are reported to be guilty of a "very grievous" but unspecified sin (Genesis 18:20, KJV; see also 13:13). Therefore, the LORD tells Abraham, he is going to destroy those cities. Among the residents of Sodom are Abraham's nephew Lot, and Lot's wife and two daughters, none of whom are named. Two divine messengers come to Sodom, and at the city gate, Lot greets them and invites them into his house. During the evening, all the men of Sodom surround Lot's house, and demand that he send out his guests "so that we may know them" (19:5, NRSV). They were not just trying to get better acquainted with the visitors; rather, they wanted to have sex with them.[23] Lot replied that as a host, he had responsibilities toward his visitors; instead, he offered to send out his two virgin daughters to the mob, who could do whatever they wanted to them. As the mob continued to threaten Lot, the angels rescued him and blinded the men of Sodom, rendering them powerless. Then, after the angels had helped Lot and his family escape, the LORD "rained upon Sodom and upon Gomorrah brimstone and fire" (19:24, KJV).[24]

Was Sodom's sin anal homosexual intercourse? The Bible never says so explicitly. Rather, several passages attribute Sodom's guilt to social injustice. Ezekiel put it this way, addressing personified Jerusalem: "This was the guilt of your sister Sodom: she and her daughters had pride, excess of food, and prosperous ease, but they did not aid the poor and needy" (16:49).[25] Jerusalem is often compared to Sodom and is condemned, because its inhabitants, called "rulers of Sodom" and "people of Gomorrah," did not "seek justice, rescue the oppressed, defend the orphan, plead for the widow" (Isaiah 1:10, 17). The story of Lot narrates a specific example of Sodom's lack of social justice: inhospitality to strangers.

The only biblical condemnation of Sodom for the intended rape of Lot's visitors is in the New Testament. As a warning to his audience, the author of the letter of Jude recalls earlier divine punishment of sinners, including the men of Sodom and Gomorrah. Just like the angels ("the sons of god") who had intercourse with human women,[26] they wanted to have sex with angels, beings other than their own kind: They "went after other flesh" (Jude 7, my translation), and were punished with eternal fire. No matter that the men of Sodom didn't know that their intended victims were angels: Ignorance is no excuse. Many translations of "other flesh" interpret it as implicitly meaning homosexual relationships, but in context this is less likely.[27]

Interpretive translations create another problem. Nowhere in the original languages of the Bible is there a word "sodomite" derived from the name of the city of Sodom and meaning someone who practices anal sex, but it recurs repeatedly in translations. In the KJV, "sodomite(s)" occurs five times,[28] although the Hebrew words so translated literally mean "holy one(s)," perhaps a euphemism for sex workers, especially in the vicinity of sacred places.[29] In the NRSV, "sodomite" occurs twice, only in the New Testament (1 Corinthians 6:9; 1 Timothy 1:10), translating the Greek word that literally means "males who bed males," probably based on the Septuagint translation of Leviticus 18:22 and 20:13.

What does the Bible say about transgender persons?

Nothing, really. One law in Deuteronomy prohibits cross-dressing:

> A woman shall not wear a man's apparel, nor shall a man put on a woman's garment; for whoever does such things is abhorrent to the LORD your God. (22:5, NRSV)[30]

A likely explanation of this prohibition is that it seeks to avoid mixing categories as the ancient Israelites understood them. The same chapter of Deuteronomy also prohibits planting other crops in a vineyard, using an ox and a donkey as plow animals together, and wearing clothes made of both wool and linen.[31] A similar motivation probably explains, at least in part, some dietary restrictions, and also same-sex male relationships. Today, many individuals and groups who accept the Bible as authoritative scripture no longer observe these prohibitions. But when some people insist that the prohibition of cross-dressing is still binding, but do not consider the others to be, the Bible's authority is ironically undermined.

What was the status of women in ancient Israel?

As in almost all societies until modern times, the status of women in ancient Israel was one of subordination to men, first to their fathers and then to their husbands. As Genesis puts it in the account of punishment of the first man and the first woman: "Your husband . . . shall rule over you" (3:16, NRSV).

When a daughter was married, she was "given" by her father to her husband, who "took" her in exchange for bride-wealth. Divorce was initiated only by the husband. If a father sold his daughter as a slave, presumably because he was in financial difficulty, she became the property of the buyer, and, with some restrictions, belonged to him in perpetuity, whereas a male could be enslaved for only six years.[32]

The inferior status of women in ancient Israel is also evident in the Tenth Commandment: "You should not scheme against your neighbor's house; you should not scheme against your neighbor's wife, or his male slave, or his female slave, or his ox, or his donkey, or anything that is your neighbor's" (Exodus 20.10, my translation).[33] This commandment concerns a man's property, listed in roughly descending order of value, from real estate to livestock. A wife is thus implicitly her husband's property.[34]

According to biblical law, sons, especially the oldest son, were their father's heirs.[35] Women could share the inheritance only in exceptional circumstances.[36] If a woman made a vow, it could be nullified by her father or, if she was married, by her husband.[37]

Sometimes we even find a kind of misogyny in the Bible. The book of Proverbs asserts:

> Better to live in a desert
>   than with a quarrelsome and ill-tempered wife.
>   (21:19, NIV)[38]

And the late second-century BCE sage Sirach says, "The birth of a daughter is a loss" (22.3, NRSV).

So, Israelite society, like most others until relatively recently, was patriarchal. Women had some rights, but their status was inferior to that of men. Still, within these constraints, individual women could exercise some power, and were to be respected. The Fifth Commandment says, "Honor your father and your mother" (Exodus 20:12); if it mentioned only the father, we could attribute this simply to prevailing patriarchy, but it does include the mother, suggesting not only the essential role of women as childbearers, but also that they had some status.[39]

That status within the family is indicated in the poem with which the book of Proverbs concludes (31:10–31), the praise of a "woman of power."[40] She provides for her household, buys real estate, engages in commerce, cares for the needy, and "fears the Lord," while her husband sits at the city gates praising her to the other men sitting there.

Paralleling the importance, although subordinate, of women in the domestic sphere are their occasional public roles. As elsewhere in the ancient Near East, women were prophets.[41] Queen mothers had special power, and one queen mother, Athaliah, became the reigning monarch herself after her son,

King Ahaziah, died in battle.[42] Although the priesthood was restricted to men, women performed many subsidiary ritual functions, and were also professional mourners and leaders of celebratory songs after military victories.[43] And like Deborah and Jael in Judges 4–5, and Judith in the book named for her, they could take the lead in military actions.

What does the New Testament say about the status of women?

The New Testament writers, for whom the Jewish scriptures were authoritative, not surprisingly adopted most of the social values of ancient Israel. In their presentation of the life of Jesus, the writers generally portray women as subordinate to men. Jesus's inner circle consisted of the Twelve, all men. The Gospels of Matthew, Mark, and John each name only a few women; in John, not even the mother of Jesus is named.[44]

Still, some women did have leadership roles. At least one, Junia, is called an apostle, although she was not one of the Twelve;[45] another, Phoebe, is called a deacon,[46] and it is likely that there were other women deacons as well.[47] Some scholars have suggested that because in all four Gospels women are the first witnesses to Jesus having been raised from the dead, they became the first Christian missionaries. However, according to Mark, although instructed by the angel at the empty tomb to inform Peter and Jesus's disciples that Jesus had been raised, the women "said nothing to anyone" (16:8). Other scholars point out that women are not mentioned in Paul's list of those to whom Jesus appeared after his resurrection, nor were women present at the Last Supper or when the resurrected Jesus commissioned the eleven remaining disciples.[48]

Similarly, although women are more prominent in the Gospel of Luke than in the other Gospels, recently scholars have suggested that this is not necessarily positive: They are "models of subordinate service, excluded from the power center of the movement and from significant responsibilities."[49] This corresponds with other New Testament views of women, who are told to be subject to their husbands,[50] and to be silent in the churches.[51] In general, then, we should probably not see a radical change in the status of women in early Christianity.

What are the biblical writers' views about marriage and divorce?

Throughout the ancient Near East, including Israel, and also to some extent in the Greco-Roman world, marriages were usually arranged between male relatives of the bride and male relatives of the groom, or the groom himself. Also, in ancient Israel as elsewhere in the ancient Near East, marriage was an institution in which a man had in his household one or more wives rather than being just between one man and one woman. Many biblical heroes—such as Abraham, Jacob, Saul, David, and Solomon—had multiple wives. Most later biblical characters seem to have been monogamous, although polygamy continued to be practiced by some Jews into the second century CE, and is described as permissible in some rabbinic texts. The New Testament never explicitly prohibits polygamy, but in early Christianity, following Greek and Roman custom of the time, monogamous marriage was the norm.[52] The Qur'an allows a man to have up to four wives, and in some majority-Muslim countries this is still the practice, but in most it is either prohibited or severely restricted. The Church of Jesus Christ of Latter-day Saints allowed polygamy for several decades in the nineteenth century, but officially abandoned it in response to American law; some fundamentalist Mormons still embrace it. Finally, some Christian groups in Africa also allow polygamy.

In ancient Israelite law, divorce was possible, but could be initiated only by the husband. The New Testament writers are not consistent on the issue of divorce. For some, such as Paul and Matthew, it was permissible in some circumstances; for others, such as Mark and Luke, marriage to a divorced person was a form of adultery, because marriage was a permanent institution.[53] These differences may reflect different practices in different early Christian communities, as in Christianity today. Jesus himself seems to have been opposed to divorce, although whether that opposition was absolute is impossible to say.[54] For both Paul and Mark, divorce could also be initiated by a wife, in accord with Roman law.

What does the Bible say about abortion?

Nothing. The text most frequently cited in opposition to abortion is the commandment prohibiting murder ("Thou shalt not kill," Exodus 20:13; Deuteronomy 5:17, KJV), but applying that to abortion assumes that the ancient Israelites thought of a fetus as a human being. No evidence supports that view. One law, which concludes with the memorable phrasing "life for life, eye for eye, tooth for tooth" (Exodus 21:23–24), explicitly deals with a fetus, but it is most likely about injury to the pregnant woman, which is to be punished according to the actual harm she suffered. Other biblical passages, describing divine providence choosing or protecting those not yet born or even conceived, are often quoted, usually by abortion opponents, even though they are not directly relevant.[55]

What does the Bible say about slavery?

As elsewhere in the ancient world, and in most societies until relatively modern times, slavery was acceptable. Slavery is even enshrined in the Ten Commandments.[56] In ancient Israel, slaves could be either non-Israelites, such as war captives and immigrants, whose status as slaves was usually permanent, or fellow Israelites, who could be enslaved in payment of a debt, but for a limited period, unless they chose to remain slaves.[57]

The same acceptance of slavery continues in the New Testament. Jesus is never quoted as being opposed to slavery. When Paul writes to Philemon about Onesimus, probably a slave of Philemon who had run away, he urges him to forgive him, but does not explicitly urge that he free him.[58] Christian slaves are instructed to obey, honor, and even love their masters, even if they are harshly treated.[59]

With these biblical precedents, in the debates about the abolition of slavery in the United States, proslavery advocates had a much better case appealing to the Bible in support of their views; abolitionists had to rely on vaguer concepts like love of neighbor and the Golden Rule. And, when slavery was finally abolished, divergence from clear biblical law and teaching on the subject of slavery significantly undercut the Bible's authority more generally, especially in the United States.

What does the Bible say about capital punishment?

Modern opponents of the death penalty cite as absolute the commandment "Thou shalt not kill" (Exodus 20:13; Deuteronomy 5:17, KJV). This is misguided, both because it is inconsistent with the many explicitly divinely given laws in which capital punishment is ordained, including "life for life," and also because the Hebrew verb used in the commandment almost always means murder, not simply killing.

Nowhere in the Bible is capital punishment categorically objected to, although from time to time we find appeals to mercy over strict justice.[60] In the Hebrew Bible, the death penalty is prescribed for many offenses, including murder, idolatry, adultery, bestiality, and cursing one's parents, but it was not always enforced. Few modern societies would enforce it for most of those offenses, and more and more have simply abolished it.

Is the New Testament anti-Semitic?

Ironically, although Christians include the Jewish scriptures in their Bibles and Jesus himself was Jewish, throughout Christian history Christians have exhibited prejudice toward Jews, all too often with horrible consequences. This prejudice both begins in and builds on the New Testament.

The most prominent example of anti-Semitism in the New Testament is the Gospel of John. In it, although Jesus observes the principal Jewish holy days, the writer has him speak as though he were not Jewish; for example, he speaks to his Jewish audience about "your law" (8:17; 10:34; see also 15:25). Moreover, he says to "the Jews," "You are from your father, the devil" (8:31, 44). Some scholars have argued that the Greek word usually translated "Jew" actually means "Judean"— someone from Judea; in some contemporaneous texts that is what it means, but this is not always so, and in any case, the earlier sense is what has informed Christian anti-Semitism.[61]

One of the charges explicitly laid against Jews in several books of the New Testament is that they were responsible for the death of Jesus. The earliest text that states this is 1 Thessalonians, in which Paul asserts that "the Jews . . . killed the Lord Jesus" (2:14–15, NIV),[62] and similar statements are found in all the Gospels and in Acts. Historically that is largely inaccurate: Jesus was executed by Roman authorities, although perhaps with the collaboration of some Jewish leaders. But according to the Gospel of Matthew, when the Roman prefect Pontius Pilate appeared willing to release Jesus, "All the people answered, 'Let his blood be on us and our children'" (27:25, NIV), which until modern times has been a pretext for anti-Semitism: All Jews have been considered "Christ-killers."

Can only believers fully understand the Bible?

Most biblical interpretation has been carried out by believers. Jewish and Christian scholars over the ages have immensely enriched our understanding of the Bible, and they continue to do so. But beginning with the Enlightenment, many scholars examined the Bible using reason alone, without dogmatic presuppositions, and what came to be called historical criticism developed.

Few would insist that one has to be a believer to study the ancient religions of Egypt or Mesopotamia or Greece or Rome. Moreover, much of the academic study of Islam, Hinduism, Buddhism, and other living religions has been carried out by Western scholars who usually have not been adherents of the religion they study. A recent volume illustrates this. *The Jewish Annotated New Testament*[63] was written by Jewish scholars about a Christian scripture. Its audience includes not just other Jews, but also non-Jews, especially Christians, who have much to learn from a different perspective.

But it is also true that religion is not just an object of study but something lived. Believers bring to the study of their own tradition insights gained from their experience. Scholars who are believers are not necessarily disqualified from being objective. We all have presuppositions; in studying the Bible it is important to be aware of one's own presuppositions, and to consciously avoid letting them bias one's interpretation. So, a faith commitment is not necessary for interpreting the Bible, nor need it stand in the way.

Does the Bible still have authority?

In this chapter I have discussed several issues in which the Bible's authority has been appealed to in support of often contradictory positions.[64] Many more could have been added, but I think that my general point is clear: Because the Bible is an anthology of historically conditioned texts, its many authors do not always agree. In addition, because the biblical writers' perspectives were different from our own has meant that many, if not most, Jews and Christians no longer accept all of its dos and don'ts. We no longer consider binding what it says about slavery, and a rapidly growing number of us also no longer consider its pronouncements on the status of women, same-sex relationships, and capital punishment valid. Appealing to the Bible selectively, to support only some positions, inevitably diminishes its authority.

But the Bible's underlying ethic, I think, can still be used as a model. If every neighbor is to be loved, and every person is a neighbor, then every person is to be loved regardless of who they are. That, I think, is ultimately the enduring message of the difficult, dangerous, challenging, and inspiring book that we call the Bible.

NOTES

Chapter 1

1. The word "Bible" ultimately derives from the name of the city of Byblos in Lebanon (called Gebal in the Bible, and in modern Arabic Jbeil). This was a port from which papyrus (the origin of our word "paper") from Egypt was shipped to Greece, so the Greeks called papyrus *byblos* (or *biblos*), "the Byblos stuff." When pages of papyrus were bound together, these pages were then called *biblion*, "book," which eventually leads to "Bible."

2. Following frequent scholarly practice, in this book I use BCE (Before the Common Era) and CE (Common Era) for the conventional BC (Before Christ) and AD (Latin "Anno Domini," "the Year of the Lord").

3. The first-century CE Jewish historian Josephus (*Against Apion* 1.38) gives the number of books as twenty-two, the number of letters in the Hebrew alphabet, probably counting Judges and Ruth as one book and Jeremiah and Lamentations as one book.

4. Similarly, Sirach 38:34–39:1 refers to "the law of the Most High," "the wisdom of the ancients," and "prophecies," and Luke 24:44 refers to "the law of Moses, the prophets, and the psalms."

5. In a scene set in the mid-fifth century BCE, "the people . . . told Ezra the scribe to bring the scroll of the *torah* of Moses, which the Lord had commanded Israel . . . and he read from it" (Nehemiah 8:1, 3).

6. The term was first used in this sense by the Christian biblical scholar Jerome ca. 400 CE.

7. The term is also used by some ancient writers.

8. The principal collections of Pseudepigrapha are R. H. Charles, ed., *The Apocrypha and Pseudepigrapha of the Old Testament* (2 vols.; Oxford: Clarendon, 1913); James H. Charlesworth, ed., *The Old Testament Pseudepigrapha* (2 vols.; New York: Doubleday, 1983, 1985); Richard Bauckham, James R. Davila, and Alexander Panayotov, eds., *Old Testament Pseudepigrapha: More Noncanonical Scriptures* (Grand Rapids, MI: Eerdmans, 2013); and Louis H. Feldman, James L. Kugel, and Lawrence H. Schiffman, eds., *Outside the Bible: Ancient Jewish Writings Related to Scripture* (3 vols.; Philadelphia: Jewish Publication Society, 2013). The different contents of these collections shows how fluid the category of Pseudepigrapha is.

9. See Matthew 24:15.

10. The canons of other Orthodox Churches include a few other books, such as 4 Maccabees (an appendix to the Greek Orthodox canon) and other books of Esdras.

11. Luther's objections were anticipated by the late-fourth–/early-fifth-century Christian biblical scholar Jerome and others, but in both eastern and western Christianity until the Reformation, the Apocrypha were considered canonical.

12. The doctrine of purgatory was based in part on 2 Maccabees 12:45; on good works, see Tobit 4:8–10; Sirach 3:30.

Chapter 2

1. Following ordinary practice, I use the term "Israelites" for the inhabitants of ancient Israel, and "Israelis" for those of the modern state of Israel.

2. Including "Talitha cum," Mark 5:41; "Ephatha," Mark 7:34; "Abba," Mark 14:36; "Eloi, Eloi, lema sabachthani," Mark 15:34.

3. *Letter of Aristeas* 301–11; Philo, *On the Life of Moses* 2.37.

4. Luther: New Testament 1522; Old Testament and Apocrypha 1534; Rosenzweig and Buber, *Die Schrift* (1925–62); Everett Fox, *The Five Books of Moses: Genesis, Exodus, Leviticus, Numbers, Deuteronomy* (New York: Schocken, 1995) and *The Early Prophets: Joshua, Judges, Samuel, Kings* (New York: Schocken, 2014); Robert Alter, *The Hebrew Bible: A Translation with Commentary* (New York: W. W. Norton, 2018); John Goldingay, *The First Testament: A New Translation* (Downers Grove, IL: IVP Academic, 2018). See also note 5.

5. One who does is David Bentley Hart, in *The New Testament: A Translation* (New Haven: Yale University Press, 2017), 380–81.

6. Fox, *The Five Books of Moses*, 10, 13.

7. Robert Alter, *The Five Books of Moses: A Translation with Commentary* (New York: W. W. Norton, 2004), 17.

8. So Good News Bible; New American Bible, Revised Edition; compare New international Version "lay with."

9. Eugene A. Nida and Charles R. Taber, *The Theory and Practice of Translation* (Leiden: Brill, 2003 [1969]), 4.

10. For example, the traditional Hebrew text of Job 1:5, 11; 2:5, 9 uses the verb "bless," almost certainly a euphemism for "curse," because no one should curse God, not even a scribe copying a text. The parallelism in the first occurrence makes this clear, as does the similar substitution in 1 Kings 21:10, 13; Psalm 10:3.

11. See Matthew 28:2; Luke 24:4, 23.

12. The addition is based on passages like 1 Chronicles 29:11. Other major additions to the original text of the New Testament include the account of Jesus refusing to condemn an adulterous woman (John 7:53–8:11) and the "Johannine Comma" (1 John 5:7–8).

13. The KJV translators were meticulous in indicating words in their translation that were not in the original texts; they indicated these words by using italics, which are sometimes misinterpreted as indicating emphasis.

14. *The Holy Scriptures According to the Masoretic Text: A New Translation* (Philadelphia: Jewish Publication Society, 1917). For antecedents, see Leonard Greenspoon, "Jewish Translations of the Bible," in Adele Berlin and Marc Zvi Brettler, eds., *The Jewish Study Bible*, 2nd ed. (New York: Oxford University Press, 2014), 2096–99.

15. *Tanakh: A New Translation of the Holy Scriptures According to the Traditional Hebrew Text* (Philadelphia: Jewish Publication Society, 1985).

16. Both words are also used of male animals, as in Genesis 6:19.

17. The Septuagint uses the word *parthenos*, which usually, although not always, means "virgin."

18. Romans 3:22, 26; Galatians 2:16; Philippians 3:9; see also Galatians 2:20; Ephesians 3:12.

Chapter 3

1. Sometimes scholars subdivide verses; for example, Genesis 2:4 has been subdivided into Genesis 2:4a and 2:4b.

2. Actually, Samuel and Kings together were probably originally one book, too (as their title in the Septuagint, 1–4 Reigns,

implies). Thus, 1 Kings opens with a continuation of the story of David's life, which began in 1 Samuel 16.

3. See especially Psalms 74:12–17; 89:8–12; 104:5–9; Job 38:4–11.

4. See Genesis 2:2; Psalms 89:5; Job 38:7.

5. Korah was a cousin of Moses and Aaron. Psalms 50 and 73–83 are attributed to Asaph, and Psalm 88 to Heman; Psalms 42–49 and 84, 85, 87, and 88 are attributed to "the sons of Korah."

6. Man of God: Hebrew *ish elohim*; seer: *hozeh* and *roeh*; one called: *nabi*.

7. See Matthew 21:46; Mark 11:32; Acts 13:1; 21:9; 1 Corinthians 12:28.

8. The "Priene Calendar Inscription," actually a composite of fragments of the same text from several sites in Asia Minor; see Craig A. Evans, "Mark's Incipit and the Priene Calendar Inscription: From Jewish Gospel to Greco-Roman Gospel," *Journal of Greco-Roman Christianity and Judaism* 1 (2000), 68–69.

9. See also Romans 1:1–4; 1 Corinthians 1:17; Galatians 2:7; 2 Timothy 1:10.

10. Many versions of "gospel parallels" that arrange them side by side are available. The most comprehensive is Arthur J. Dewey and Robert J. Miller, *The Complete Gospel Parallels* (Salem, OR: Polebridge, 2012).

11. Recently some scholars have suggested an early second-century date; see Dennis E. Smith and Joseph B. Tyson, eds., *Acts and Christian Beginnings: The Acts Seminar Report* (Salem, OR: Polebridge, 2013), page xx.

12. See Acts 16:10–17; 20:5–15; 21:1–18; 27:1–28:16.

13. See Colossians 4:16; 1 Thessalonians 5:27.

14. See also Galatians 6:11; Colossians 4:18; 2 Thessalonians 3:17; if the latter two letters are pseudonymous, as some scholars think (see page 54), then the claim that the note is by Paul himself is an imitation of his practice.

Chapter 4

1. See further the discussion of the Pseudepigrapha on page 6.

2. See also Exodus 34:27–28; Numbers 33:2; Deuteronomy 31:9, 24.

3. The Hebrew word *sefer*, usually translated "book," more accurately means "scroll."

4. Quotations of "the book (of the law) of Moses" are also found in 2 Kings 14:6; 2 Chronicles 35:12; Nehemiah 13:1.

5. See, for example, Mark 1:44 ; 7:10; 12:19; and also 1 Corinthians 9:9; 2 Corinthians 3:15; Hebrews 10:28.

6. For example, 2 Chronicles 29:30; 4 Maccabees 18:15; Mark 12:36; Acts 2:25; Romans 4:6.
7. See 1 Samuel 16:14–23; 2 Samuel 1:17–27. In ancient Israel, as elsewhere in the ancient world, poetry was frequently sung.
8. Psalm 2, in Acts 4:25–26 (also not attributed to David in the Septuagint), and Psalm 95, in Hebrews 4:7.
9. b. Pesahim 117a; b. Baba Batra 14b–15a; Midrash Tehillim 1:2.
10. 1 Kings 10:10.
11. 1 Kings 10:22.
12. The title of the book in the Masoretic Text is "The Song of Songs which is of Solomon" (my translation), using the same preposition that is used of David in the superscriptions to many psalms. It could mean either "by Solomon" or "concerning Solomon."
13. 1 Kings 11:3.
14. See further pages 101–2.
15. 13:23; compare 2 Corinthians 1:1.
16. The second-century exegete Origin reportedly said, "Who wrote the epistle, in truth, only God knows" (Eusebius, *Ecclesiastical History* 6.25.14).
17. See Mark 6:3; Galatians 1:19.
18. The number of the Twelve, often called the twelve apostles, is consciously based on Jacob's twelve sons, the ancestors of the twelve tribes of Israel.
19. The Greek style of the two books is very different. That of the Gospel of John has been called "clear and accurate," while that of Revelation is "idiosyncratic" and "peculiar" (Craig R. Koester, "Revelation, Book of," in K. D. Sakenfeld, ed., *The New Interpreter's Dictionary of the Bible*, Vol. 4 [Nashville, TN: Abingdon, 2009]), 789, 796.
20. Hebrew *torah*.
21. See Jeremiah 52:4–30; 43:5–7.
22. 2 Kings 22:8–13.

Chapter 5
1. See Jeremiah 52:28–30; Matthew 2:19–23.
2. In antiquity the elevation of the Dead Sea averaged about a hundred feet higher than at present; water consumption both east and west of the Jordan River has drastically reduced its flow, so that the Dead Sea has begun to dry up.
3. For example, Ezra 1:3; Luke 10:30.

4. Jerusalem is also called Jebus (Joshua 15:8; 18:28; Judges 19:10; 1 Chronicles 11:4), and Hebron is also called Kiriath-arba (for example, Genesis 23:2; Joshua 14:15; see also Nehemiah 11:25). In Arabic, the name of Jerusalem is el-Quds ("the Holy [city]"), and that of Hebron is el-Khalil ("the Friend"), referring to Abraham as "the friend of God" (see Isaiah 41:8; 2 Chronicles 20:7; Qur'an 4.125).

5. See Genesis 2:8; 13:10; Isaiah 51:3; Ezekiel 28:13; 31:8–9.

6. Caiaphas's name also probably occurs on an ossuary, a coffin for bones, discovered in Jerusalem in the late twentieth century.

7. The earliest nonbiblical mention of David is in a ninth-century BCE victory stela by an Aramean king from Tel Dan in northern Israel, which mentions "the house of David."

8. In the stela, Israel is mentioned together with Canaan, and several city-states in Canaan, but unlike them Israel is identified specifically as a foreign people.

9. Michael D. Coogan and Mark S. Smith, ed. and trans., *Stories from Ancient Canaan*, 2nd ed. (Louisville, KY: Westminster John Knox, 2012), 114.

10. See Sirach 34:12–13; also 39:4.

11. 6.146–49.

12. For a reconstruction of life in an Israelite village based on a synthesis of archaeological and biblical data, see "A Day in Micah's Household" in Philip J. King and Lawrence E. Stager, *Life in Biblical Israel* (Louisville, KY: Westminster John Knox, 2001), 12–19. For the Roman period, see Jodi Magness, *Stone and Dung, Oil and Spit: Jewish Daily Life in the Time of Jesus* (Grand Rapids, MI: Eerdmans, 2011).

13. See Ezekiel 40:6–37.

14. See 1 Kings 6:38–7:1.

15. For descriptions of the cherubim, see Exodus 25:18–22; 1 Kings 6:23–28; Ezekiel 10:14, and compare Ezekiel 1:4–28; 41:18–19.

16. See also 1 Samuel 4:4; Psalms 80:1; 132:7.

17. See also 1 Chronicles 28:2; Psalms 132:7; Lamentations 2:1. Descriptions of the ark of the covenant in the Pentateuch and 1 and 2 Samuel come from different sources, at least some of which describe the ark that was installed in the Temple.

18. 2 Kings 25:13–17; Jeremiah 52:17–23.

19. 2 Maccabees 2:4–7.

20. Translation by Christopher Rollston, "Siloam Inscription and Hezekiah's Tunnel." http://bibleodyssey.org/en/places/

related-articles/siloam-inscription-and-hezekiahs-tunnel. One
cubit is about 1.5 feet.

21. In "The Date of the Siloam Tunnel Reconsidered," *Tel Aviv* 38
(2011), 147–157, Ronny Reich and Eli Shukron suggest that the
tunnel was constructed several decades before Hezekiah began
to rule. In "The Why, How, and When of the Siloam Tunnel
Reevaluated," *Bulletin of the American Schools of Oriental Research*
359 (August 2010), 57–65, Amihai Sneh, Ram Weinberger, and
Eyal Shalev argue that it was constructed during the reign of
Hezekiah's successor, Manasseh. John Rogerson and Philip
R. Davies, in "Was the Siloam Tunnel Built by Hezekiah?" *Biblical
Archaeologist* 59 (1996), 138–49, propose a second-century BCE date.

22. For example, Bryant Wood asserts that "the archaeological
evidence supports the historical accuracy of the biblical account
in every detail" (https://answersingenesis.org/archaeology/
the-walls-of-jericho/). Contrast Maura Sala, who says that "no
archaeological evidence corroborates the biblical account of what
happened in Jericho" (http://www.bibleodyssey.org/places/
related-articles/walls-of-jericho.aspx).

Chapter 6

1. For example, Exodus 31:18.
2. 2 Kings 8:26; 11:1–16.
3. See further pages 121–22.
4. See further pages 107–8.
5. For similar sayings, see Matthew 18:3; Mark 9:33–37; Luke 9:48.
6. Translations of the Gospel of Thomas in this section are by
Stephen Patterson and Marvin Meyer, in *The Gnostic Society
Library, The Nag Hammadi Library, The Gospel of Thomas*, http://
gnosis.org/naghamm/gosthom.html.
7. 11:16; 20:24; 21:2.
8. One of the brothers of Jesus was named Judas (Mark 6:3), but he
and Thomas are never equated.
9. See page 172, n. 9.
10. The Synoptics mention only one trip to Jerusalem, for Passover;
in John, three Passovers are mentioned (2:13; 6:4; 11:55).
11. 6:35, 48; 8:12; 9:5; 10:11, 14; 11:25.
12. Romans 1:3 speaks of Jesus as "descended from David according to
the flesh," which, following the usual genealogical pattern, would
be through his father, Joseph, as in Matthew 1:16 and Luke 3:23.

13. See also Matthew 2:2, 9, alluding to Numbers 24:17; Matthew 2:6, quoting Micah 5:2; Matthew 2:11, alluding to Isaiah 60:6 and Psalm 72:11; Matthew 2:15, quoting Hosea 11:1; and Matthew 2:20, alluding to Exodus 4:19.
14. Luke 1:47–55; 1 Samuel 2:1–10.
15. In John 2:13–22 this is set at the beginning of Jesus's ministry, but the details are close to those found in the Synoptic Gospels.
16. In the Synoptic Gospels, this is a Passover meal; in John it is not, because in John's chronology Passover begins on Friday.
17. Called Gethsemane ("oil-garden") in Matthew 26:36; Mark 14:32.
18. See also Matthew 27:35; Mark 15:24; Luke 23:34. On Jesus being mocked, compare Psalm 22:6–8 and Matthew 27:39, Mark 15:29; on his thirst, Psalm 22:15 (and 69:21), John 19:28. Other fulfillment formulae occur in Matthew 21:4–5, 16, 42; 26:24, 31, 54, 56; 27:9–10; Mark 12:10; 14:21, 27, 49; Luke 22:37; 24:27, 44–47; John 12:14–16, 38–41; 13:18; 19:28, 36, 37.
19. For example, 2 Maccabees 6–7; 4 Maccabees 5–17; *Apocalypse of Elijah* 4; *Martyrdom and Ascension of Isaiah 1–5*; *Lives of the Prophets*, according to which Isaiah (1:1), Jeremiah (2:1), Ezekiel (3:2), Micah (6:2), Amos (7:1–3), and Zechariah (23:1) were all martyred; see also Hebrews 11:37.

Chapter 7

1. Published by De Gruyter (Berlin: 2009–), which also publishes *The Journal of the Bible and Its Reception*, along with handbooks and monographs on the same topic. Not surprisingly, the editorial board of this massive project has changed considerably since its inception; see https://www.degruyter.com/view/supplement/s20269_Editorial_Board.pdf for a list of current and former editors.
2. Two recent commentaries that explicitly include reception history in their treatment are Samuel E. Balentine, *Job* (Macon, GA: Smith and Helwys, 2006) and C. L. Seow, *Job 1–21: Interpretation and Commentary* (Grand Rapids, MI: Wm. B. Eerdmans, 2013). See also Mark Larrimore, *The Book of Job: A Biography* (Princeton, NJ: Princeton University Press, 2013.
3. Ezekiel 14:14, 20. Danel is not the same person as Daniel, the hero of the biblical book named for him, but a character in the Ugaritic epic *Aqhat*, probably also mentioned in Ezekiel 28:3.
4. 1:6; 2:1; 38:7. See further page 123.
5. University Park: Pennsylvania State University Press, 1996.

6. *A Journey of Two Psalms: The Reception of Psalms 1 and 2 in Jewish and Christian Tradition* (Oxford: Oxford University Press, 2014).

7. "Biblical Studies on Holiday? A Personal View of Reception History," in *Reception History and Biblical Studies: Theory and Practice* (ed. E. England and W. J. Lyons; London: T&T Clark, 2015), 17–44.

8. By "promiscuous" he apparently means "mixed" (that is, consisting of both males and females). Quotations from the Webster Bible are from biblestudytools.com/wbt/.

9. For example, 1 Samuel 25:22; 1 Kings 14:10. NJPS has a textual note: "Lit[erally] "one who pees against a wall.""

10. See Jeffrey D. Smoak, *The Priestly Blessing in Inscription and Scripture: The Early History of Numbers 6:24–26* (New York: Oxford University Press, 2015), especially pages 1–3.

11. Leviticus 23:42–43.

12. Exodus 12:1–6; see also Ezekiel 45:21.

13. Leviticus 23:27.

14. Exodus 23:16; 34:22. In the Bible, the Hebrew phrase *rosh hashanah* occurs only in Ezekiel 40:1, referring to the Day of Atonement; compare Leviticus 23:27. It is worth noting that we also have competing calendars; although New Year's Day is January 1, the preceding months are named the seventh, eighth, ninth, and tenth (September, October, November, and December), names based on a Roman spring New Year on March 1.

15. See 2 Kings 25:8; Jeremiah 52:12; b. Ta'anit 29a.

16. 1 Maccabees 4:36–59.

17. These dates follow the Gregorian calendar. Various Christian Orthodox churches have different dates because they follow different versions of the Julian calendar.

18. Because the traditional Jewish calendar and the modern Western calendar are not synchronized, Passover and Easter do not usually coincide exactly.

19. Acts 1:3–11; 2:1. Pentecost was originally the Jewish festival of Weeks (Shavuot).

20. See Genesis 2:2–3; Exodus 16:29–30; Exodus 20:11; etc. There are no good nonbiblical parallels to the Sabbath observance.

21. See, for example, Amos 8:5; Nehemiah 10:31; 13:15; and also Jeremiah 17:21–27, where "burden" probably means "merchandise."

22. See, for example, Numbers 15:32–36.

23. Exodus 35:3; 16:23.

24. See, for example, Exodus 31:14; 35:2.
25. For an early elaboration, see *Jubilees* 50.
26. 1 Maccabees 2:29–41.
27. This phrase explains the etymology of the name of Sunday in the Romance languages (*Domenica*, etc., from the Latin word *Dominus*, "Lord").
28. See also Acts 20:7; 1 Corinthians 16:2.
29. Genesis 17:10.
30. Matthew 28:19; 1 Corinthians 11:24–25.
31. For example, Proverbs 8:15–16; Wisdom of Solomon 6:3; John 19:11; 1 Peter 2:13–14.
32. See also John 20:23. Interestingly, Matthew 16:19 and 18:18 are the only two places in all four Gospels where the word "church" (Greek *ekklesia*) occurs.
33. See Galatians 2:7–9, 11–14.
34. For example, Isaiah 62:8; Psalm 144:8; Daniel 12:7; see also Genesis 14:22; Exodus 6:8; Numbers 14:30.
35. See also James 5:12, and compare Matthew 23:20–22.
36. Genesis 24:2–9; 47:29–31.
37. See also Genesis 46:26; Judges 8:30.
38. https://news.gallup.com/poll/21814/evolution-creationism-intelligent-design.aspx.
39. See 2 Kings 5:1–14; 20:1–7; Mark 3:10.
40. For example, Leviticus 13:1–46; Mark 1:40–44.
41. King Asa of Judah is criticized because when he was ill, he consulted physicians but did not ask for divine help (2 Chronicles 16:12)
42. Literal translation; the same word is also used in Matthew 4:24. Most translations interpret the word to mean "epileptic." But moonstroke is attested elsewhere in the Bible (see Psalm 121:6) and the ancient Near East. Note also both the etymology of the term "lunacy" (from Latin *luna*, "moon") and its vagueness.

Chapter 8

1. Genesis 4:26 (J).
2. Exodus 3:15 (E); 6:2–3 (P). In part because of these traditions, many scholars have suggested that Yahweh was originally the deity of Moses's non-Israelite in-laws, whom Moses adopted while living with them in Midian in northern Arabia (see Exodus 3:1). Some nonbiblical evidence supports this theory, as do texts such as Judges 5:4 and Deuteronomy 33:2.

3. In any case, the name is connected with the verb "to be," as the alternate forms "I am" and "I am who I am" (Exodus 3:14) indicate.

4. The name "Jehovah" comes from a medieval misreading of the Masoretic Text, in which the consonants *yhwh* are combined with the vowels of *adonay*.

5. Hebrew *yhwh hu' ha'elohim*, for example Deuteronomy 4:35; 1 Kings 18:39. The related words *El* and *Eloah* are also usually translated "God."

6. Hebrew *yhwh tseba'ot*; compare Sabaoth in Latin (in the "Sanctus") and English (twice in the KJV).

7. For example, Exodus 15:11; Psalms 86:8; 89:6.

8. For example, Genesis 1:26; 3:22; 11:7; Isaiah 6:8; see also 1 Kings 22:19; Psalm 82:1.

9. Psalms 29:1; 82:6; 89:6; Job 1:6; 2:1; 38:7; only in the highly mythological context of Genesis 6:2 do most translations render the phrase literally. On Deuteronomy 32:8, see page 21.

10. See, for example, Judges 3:7; 2 Kings 23:5–7, 13; Ezekiel 8:14. For a complete list, see Karel van der Toorn, Bob Becking, and Pieter W. van der Horst, eds., *Dictionary of Deities and Demons in the Bible* (2nd ed.; Leiden: Brill, and Grand Rapids, MI: Eerdmans, 1999).

11. See also Isaiah 43:11; 44:6; 45:5, 21; 46:9. Similar language is used in Deuteronomy 32:39, which may also date to the sixth century BCE.

12. See Isaiah 10:5–6.

13. For example, Wisdom of Solomon 2:12–13; Sirach 4:10.

14. See also Exodus 4:22; Jeremiah 31:9; Malachi 1:6.

15. Also quoted with reference to Jesus in Acts 13:33; Hebrews 1:5; 5:5. See also Psalm 89:20–26 (quoted in Acts 13.22), and Isaiah 9:6, where the divine council is welcoming a new member. In Ugaritic, a king is also called "son of El."

16. Mark 14:36.

17. Luke 11:2; Matthew 6:9 has "Our father."

18. See Genesis 6:1–4.

19. See 1:18, 34; etc.

20. See Ezekiel 2:1 and the textual note there. NRSV is probably using inclusive language in Ezekiel, but the translators seem to have been reluctant to do so in Daniel 7:13 because of its New Testament usage. The phrase is also used, for example, in Psalm 8:4, where the parallelism makes the sense clear: "What is man,

that thou art mindful of him? and the son of man, that thou visitest him?" (KJV).

21. The exceptions are Acts 7:56, in a speech by Stephen alluding to Jesus's words in Luke 22:69; Hebrews 2:6, quoting Psalm 8:4; and Revelation 1:13 and 14:14, alluding to Daniel 7:13.

22. See Mark 13:26.; 14:62.

23. The anointing could be more than just a token dab of oil; see Exodus 29:7; Psalm 133:2.

24. For example, 1 Samuel 24:6; 2 Samuel 1:14.

25. See Daniel 9:25–26. In Isaiah 45:1, the Persian king Cyrus the Great is called Yahweh's "anointed."

26. For example, 2 Samuel 7:16; Ezekiel 37:24; Hosea 1:11; Amos 9:11; Psalm 89:35–37.

27. See also Revelation 22:20; Philippians 4:5.

28. See also Matthew 10:23; Mark 13:30.

29. See 2 Peter 3:4.

30. See note 26.

31. See also Luke 1:32; Romans 1:3.

32. Matthew's genealogy begins with Abraham, and is divided into three parts of fourteen generations, perhaps because the Hebrew consonants of the name David have numerical equivalents based on their position in the Hebrew alphabet: $d = 4$ and v $(w) = 6$, so $4 + 6 + 4 = 14$. Luke's genealogy is in reverse order and traces Jesus's ancestor ultimately back to Adam, called "son of God" (3:38).

33. Micah 5:2, quoted in Matthew 2:5–6. But see also John 7:40–43.

34. For example, Genesis 31:44 (boundary dispute); 1 Kings 5:12 (treaty); Malachi 2:14 (marriage).

35. See Genesis 15; 31:44–54; Exodus 24:3–8; Jeremiah 34:18–20.

36. Genesis 9:8–17.

37. Genesis 15:18–21.

38. Genesis 17:1–14.

39. The Ten Commandments, also known as the Decalogue, are found in two slightly different versions in Exodus 20:2–17 and Deuteronomy 5:6–21. The phrase "ten words" occurs in Exodus 34:28; Deuteronomy 4:13; 10:4. Examples of the rewards ("blessings") and punishments ("curses") are found in Leviticus 26 and Deuteronomy 28.

40. See 2 Samuel 7:12–16; 23:5; Psalm 89:28–37. The only exception is Psalm 132:12.

41. "This cup is the new covenant in my blood," Luke 22:20; 1 Corinthians 11:25. In some manuscripts it is also found in Matthew 26:28 and Mark 14:24, although the better reading is probably "my blood of the covenant," probably alluding to Exodus 24:8 and Zechariah 9:11.
42. Note the occurrence of part of this formulation in the Decalogue (Exodus 20:5–6; Deuteronomy 5:9–10).
43. See also Tobit 4:17, but condemned in Deuteronomy 26:14.
44. On Saul and the medium, see 1 Samuel 28:3–25, and also the criticism of Saul for having consulted her in 1 Chronicles 10:13–14. For condemnation of necromancy, see Leviticus 19:31; 20:6, 27; Deuteronomy 18:10–11; Isaiah 8:19–20; see also Isaiah 29:4.
45. The word "god" translates Hebrew *elohim* (see page 87). The words "the earth" frequently mean "the underworld." The word *elohim* is also used of the dead in Isaiah 8:19. In the very difficult Psalm 16:3–4, "the holy ones" may also refer to the dead.
46. Genesis 5:24; 2 Kings 2:11. Jesus's ascension into heaven (Acts 1:9) is another literary connection between Jesus and Elijah (see page 76).
47. The probable etymology of the word *sheol* is from a verb meaning "to ask," because Sheol is never satisfied; see Proverbs 30:16; Isaiah 5:14; Habakkuk 2:5.
48. See, for example, Job 3:13–19; 7:9; 24:19; Psalm 89:48.
49. See also Psalms 30:9; 88:10–12; 115:17; Isaiah 38:18.
50. See 2 Maccabees 7:9; 12:43–45; 3 Maccabees 18:23.
51. See Mark 12:18–27; Acts 23:8; Josephus, *Antiquities* 18.16.
52. Acts 9:1–9; 22:6–11; 26:12–18.
53. Luke 24:37.
54. See especially 12:10–13:1, and also 15:13–14.
55. The same is true of the end of the Christian canon of the Old Testament, which ends with a reference to the laws God gave to Moses (Malachi 4:4).
56. 5:15; 15:15; 16:12; 24:18, 22; and variations too many to list.
57. Luke 9:31. NRSV translates the Greek word *exodos* as "departure."
58. See John 1:29; 19:36, quoting Exodus 12:46.

Chapter 9

1. Whether Rabbi Hillel actually said this is as difficult as determining whether Jesus said everything that he is reported to have said.

2. See also Luke 6:31. The popular version of this "Golden Rule" is "Do unto others as you would have them do unto you."

3. See also Mark 12:29–31; Luke 10:27–28.

4. See also Romans 13:8–10.

5. See also Jerusalem Talmud Nedarim 9.3.41; Genesis Rabbah 24.27.

6. In Leviticus 19:18, the word "neighbor" is synonymous with the phrase "any of your people" (NRSV; literally, "the sons of your people").

7. See also Deuteronomy 10:19. The same Hebrew word (*ger*) is used in both verses, although NRSV translates it in the second as "stranger."

8. On the status of resident aliens/immigrants in ancient Israel, see Michael Coogan, *God's Favorites: Judaism, Christianity, and the Myth of Divine Chosenness in Judaism and Christianity* (Boston: Beacon, 2019), 115–16.

9. One of the very few sayings of Jesus that the controversial Jesus Seminar marked in red, meaning that "Jesus undoubtedly said this or something very like it" (Robert W. Funk, Roy W. Hoover, and the Jesus Seminar, *The Five Gospels: The Search for the Authentic Words of Jesus* [New York: Macmillan, 1993], 36; see page 549 for the complete list of red sayings, some fifteen in all not counting parallels).

10. See also Proverbs 25:21; Luke 10:25–37.

11. See also Leviticus 19:9–10; 23:22.

12. *Summa Theologica* 2.2.32. Matthew has "caring for the sick" and "visiting those in prison" for the fifth and sixth items; burying the dead is taken from the example of Tobit (Tobit 1:17).

13. See also James 1:27; 2:14–17.

14. Literally, "does not lift up faces"; cf. KJV: "regardeth not persons."

15. See for example Deuteronomy 20:16–17; Joshua 6:21; 10:40; 11:14–15. On the divine attitude toward animals, contrast Jonah 4:11.

16. *to'ebah*. The same translation is used for other words that have a similar sense.

17. Although Leviticus 18:9 forbids a man having sexual intercourse with his sister or half-sister (see also Ezekiel 22:11), at least sometimes such a relationship was possible (see Genesis 20:12; 2 Samuel 13:11–13).

18. See Leviticus 11:7, 10–12; Deuteronomy 14:3, 8, 10. Other dietary prohibitions are found in those passages and elsewhere in the

Hebrew Bible. The origin of these prohibitions is disputed.
Certainly cultural preferences play a role: In some modern
cultures, cat, dog, and horse meat are regularly eaten, while in
others they are not.

19. 1 Samuel 18:1–4; 20:41.

20. See John 13:23, 25.

21. Literal translation. NRSV has "sodomites" in both verses. KJV
    has "abusers of themselves with mankind" in the first and "them
    that defile themselves with mankind" in the second. NABRE
    has "sodomites" in the first and "practicing homosexuals" in the
    second. See further page 148.

22. 1 Corinthians 11:14.

23. See page 17.

24. A variant of this story occurs in Judges 19. Again strangers come
    to a town, this time the Israelite town of Gibeah, and are taken in;
    again the men of the town surround the host's house demanding
    that his guest be sent out "so that we may know him"; again the
    host offers them two women (in this case, his virgin daughter
    and his guest's secondary wife). But this time no angels came to
    the rescue, and the guest's wife was gang-raped all night.

25. See also Matthew 10:14–15, and, more generally, Wisdom of
    Solomon 19:13–17.

26. Genesis 6:1–4.

27. For example, "unnatural lust" (NRSV); "perversion" (NIV).

28. Deuteronomy 23:17; 1 Kings 14:24; 15:12; 22:46; 2 Kings 23:7.

29. Note the use of the same word to mean "prostitute" in Genesis
    38:21 (compare verse 15). Twentieth-century translations
    preferred to translate the Hebrew word as "(male) temple
    prostitute(s)" or "cult prostitute(s)," but more recently scholars
    have concluded that sacred prostitution did not exist in ancient
    Israel. CEB translates the word as "consecrated worker(s),"
    which is linguistically accurate if overly expansive.

30. The Hebrew word translated "abhorrent" is often translated
    "abomination"; see page 145.

31. Deuteronomy 22:9–11; see also Leviticus 19:19.

32. Exodus 21:7–11; compare 21:2.

33. The Hebrew word usually translated "covet" means more than
    just "desire"; CEB implies this when it translates the second
    occurrence of the verb as "desire and try to take." See further
    Michael Coogan, *The Ten Commandments: A Short History of an
    Ancient Text* (New Haven: Yale University Press, 2014), 90–92.

34. The variant of this commandment in Deuteronomy 5:21 puts the wife before the other property, but this does not really change her status.
35. See Deuteronomy 21:15–17.
36. As when a father had no sons, like Zelophehad, whose daughters petitioned Moses that they inherit his portion of the Promised Land (Numbers 27:1–11; see also 36:1–12; Joshua 17:3–6). Job's daughters, who are named, share their father's inheritance with his unnamed sons (Job 42:13–15), but these are fictional characters, and also non-Israelites.
37. Numbers 30:3–15.
38. A variant proverb in 21:9 has "on the corner of a roof" for "in a desert." See also Proverbs 19:13; 27:15–16.
39. Note also the pairing of father and mother in other laws (for example, Exodus 21:15; Deuteronomy 27:16), in the book of Proverbs (for example, 1:8; 6:20; 19:26), and elsewhere. See further Cynthia R. Chapman, *The House of the Mother: The Social Roles of Maternal Kin in Biblical Hebrew Narrative and Poetry* (New Haven: Yale University Press, 2016).
40. Proverbs 31:10–31. The usual translations of the opening words ("capable wife," NRSV, New Jewish Publication Society Translation; "woman of worth," NABRE) dilute the literal sense.
41. Four are named: Miriam (Exodus 15:20), Deborah (Judges 4:4), Huldah (2 Kings 22:14), and Noadiah (Nehemiah 6:14). See also Isaiah 8:3; Ezekiel 13:17; Joel 2:28; Luke 2:36.
42. Notable queen mothers are Bathsheba (1 Kings 2:13–25) and Jezebel (2 Kings 9:30–37). On Athaliah, see 2 Kings 11:1–3.
43. On women's ritual functions, see for example, Exodus 35:25–26; 38:8; 1 Samuel 2:22; 2 Kings 23:7. On women as mourners, see 2 Chronicles 35:25; Jeremiah 9:17–18; Ezekiel 32:16. On women as singers of victory songs, see Exodus 15:20–21; Judges 11:34; 1 Samuel 18:6–7.
44. On the mother of Jesus in John, see 2:1–12; 19:25–27; also 6:42.
45. Romans 16:7.
46. Romans 16:1.
47. That is a possible interpretation of 1 Timothy 3:11 in its immediate context, but is inconsistent with 2:11–12.
48. 1 Corinthians 15:5–8; Mark 14:17; Matthew 28:16–20.
49. Jane D. Schaberg and Sharon H. Ringe, "The Gospel of Luke," in *Women's Bible Commentary* (C. A. Newsom, S. H. Ringe, and J.

E. Lapsley, eds.; Louisville, KY: Westminster John Knox, 3rd ed., 2012), 493.

50. Ephesians 5:22–24, echoing Genesis 3:16; see also 1 Corinthians 11:3; Colossians 3:18; Titus 2:5; 1 Peter 3:1–6.

51. 1 Corinthians 14:34–35; see also 1 Timothy 2:11–12.

52. Monogamy may be presented as an ideal for bishops and deacons in 1 Timothy 3:2. 12, where they are instructed to be the "husband of one wife," but this could also refer to remarriage after divorce or the death of a spouse.

53. 1 Corinthians 7:12–13; Matthew 19:9; Mark 10:11–12; Luke 16:18.

54. Note especially Paul's reference to Jesus's view in 1 Corinthians 7:10.

55. For example, Isaiah 49:1, 5; Jeremiah 1:5; Psalm 139:13–16; Galatians 1:15.

56. See Exodus 20:10, 17; Deuteronomy 5:14, 21.

57. On war captives and other non-Israelite slaves, see, for example, Leviticus 25:44–46; Numbers 31:26–47; Deuteronomy 20:14; on fellow-Israelite slaves, see Exodus 21:2–6; Leviticus 25:39–43.

58. 1 Corinthians 7:17, 21–24 is similarly ambiguous.

59. See Ephesians 6:5–8; 1 Timothy 6:1–2; Titus 2:9–10; 1 Peter 2:18–25.

60. Note the example of God's protection of Cain, who had murdered his brother Abel (Genesis 4:8–15), and the more general statement that God takes no pleasure in the death of the wicked (Ezekiel 33:11); see also Matthew 5:38–39.

61. For a discussion of the term, see Joshua D. Garroway, "*Ioudaios*," in *The Jewish Annotated New Testament* (ed. A.-J. Levine and M. Z. Brettler; New York: Oxford University Press, 2nd ed., 2017), 596–99.

62. Who precisely Paul means by "the Jews" is unclear (see previous note), especially since Paul himself was Jewish.

63. New York: Oxford University Press, 2011, 2017.

64. Even "the Devil can cite Scripture for his purpose," Shakespeare observed (*The Merchant of Venice*, 1.3.99).

FURTHER READING

General

Coogan, Michael D., and Cynthia R. Chapman. *The Old Testament: A Historical and Literary Introduction to the Hebrew Scriptures.* 4th ed. New York: Oxford University Press, 2018.

Ehrman, Bart D. *The New Testament: A Historical Introduction to the Early Christian Writings.* 7th ed. New York: Oxford University Press, 2019.

Freedman, David Noel, ed. *The Anchor Bible Dictionary.* 6 vols. New York: Doubleday, 1992.

Powell, Mark Allen, ed. *The HarperCollins Bible Dictionary.* 3rd ed. New York: HarperOne, 2011.

Sakenfeld, Katharine Doob, ed. *The New Interpreter's Dictionary of the Bible.* 5 vols. Nashville, TN: Abingdon, 2006–2009.

Study Bibles

Attridge, Harold W., ed. *The HarperCollins Study Bible.* Rev. ed. New York: Harper Collins, 2006. Uses New Revised Standard Version (NRSV) translation.

Berlin, Adele, and Marc Zvi Brettler, eds. *The Jewish Study Bible.* 2nd ed. New York: Oxford University Press, 2014. Uses New Jewish Publication Society Translation (NJPS).

Coogan, Michael D., ed. *The New Oxford Annotated Bible with the Apocrypha.* 5th ed. New York: Oxford University Press, 2018. Uses NRSV translation.

Green, Joel B., ed. *The CEB Study Bible with Apocrypha.* Nashville, TN: Common English Bible, 2013. Uses Common English Bible (CEB) translation.

Harrelson, Walter J. *The New Interpreter's Study Bible*. Nashville, TN: Abingdon, 2003. Uses NRSV translation.

Levine, Amy-Jill, and Marc Zvi Brettler, eds. *The Jewish Annotated New Testament*. 2nd ed. New York: Oxford University Press, 2017. Uses NRSV translation.

O'Day, Gail R., and David L. Petersen, eds. *The Access Bible*. Updated ed. New York: Oxford University Press, 2011. Uses NRSV translation.

Senior, Donald, John J. Collins, and Mary Ann Getty, eds. *The Catholic Study Bible*. 3rd ed. New York: Oxford University Press, 2016. Uses New American Bible, Revised Edition (NABRE) translation.

1 Bible and Bibles

McDonald, Lee Martin. "Canon of the New Testament," pages 536–547 in *The New Interpreter's Dictionary of the Bible*, Vol. 1 (ed. K. D. Sakenfeld; Nashville, TN: Abingdon, 2006).

Trebolle, Julio. "Canon of the Old Testament," pages 548–563 in *The New Interpreter's Dictionary of the Bible*, Vol. 1 (ed. K. D. Sakenfeld; Nashville, TN: Abingdon, 2006).

2 Languages, Texts, and Translations

Fuller, Russell E. "Text Criticism, OT," pages 531–534 in *The New Interpreter's Dictionary of the Bible*, Vol. 5 (ed. K. D. Sakenfeld; Nashville, TN: Abingdon, 2009).

Holmes, Michael W. "Text Criticism, NT," pages 529–531 in *The New Interpreter's Dictionary of the Bible*, Vol. 5 (ed. K. D. Sakenfeld; Nashville, TN: Abingdon, 2009).

van Steenbergen, Gerrit J. "Translations, English," pages 435–449 in *The Oxford Encyclopedia of the Books of the Bible*, Vol. 2 (ed. M. D. Coogan; New York: Oxford University Press, 2011).

3 The Contents of the Bible

Coogan, Michael D., ed. *The Oxford Encyclopedia of the Books of the Bible*. 2 vols. New York: Oxford University Press, 2011.

4 Authors and Authorship

Hendel, Ronald, and Jan Joosten. *How Old Is the Hebrew Bible? A Linguistic, Textual, and Historical Study*. New Haven: Yale University Press, 2018.

5 The Contexts of the Bible

Aḥituv, Shmuel. *Echoes from the Past: Hebrew and Cognate Inscriptions from the Biblical Period*. Jerusalem: Carta, 2008.

Cogan, Mordechai. *Bound for Exile: Israelites and Judeans under Imperial Yoke*. Jerusalem: Carta, 2013.

Cogan, Mordechai. *The Raging Torrent: Historical Inscriptions from Assyria and Babylonia Relating to Ancient Israel*. 2nd ed. Jerusalem: Carta, 2015.

Coogan, Michael D., ed. *The Oxford History of the Biblical World*. New York: Oxford University Press, 1998; 2001.

Coogan, Michael D., ed. *A Reader of Ancient Near Eastern Texts: Sources for the Study of the Old Testament*. New York: Oxford University Press, 2013.

Curtis, Adrian, ed. *Oxford Bible Atlas*. 4th ed. Oxford: Oxford University Press, 2007.

Hallo, William W., and K. Lawson Younger, eds. *The Context of Scripture*. 4 vols. Leiden: Brill, 1997–2016.

King, Philip J., and Lawrence E. Stager. *Life in Biblical Israel*. Louisville, KY: Westminster John Knox, 2001.

Magness, Jodi. "Archaeology of the Land of Israel at the Time of Jesus," pages 599–602 in *The Jewish Annotated New Testament* (ed. A.-J. Levine and M. Z. Brettler; New York: Oxford University Press, 2nd ed., 2017).

Pritchard, James B. *Ancient Near Eastern Texts Relating to the Old Testament*. 3rd ed. Princeton, NJ: Princeton University Press, 1969.

6 Interpretive Strategies

Barton, John. *Reading the Old Testament: Method in Biblical Study*. Rev. and enlarged ed. Louisville, KY: Westminster John Knox, 1996.

Brown, Raymond E. *The Birth of the Messiah: A Commentary on the Infancy Narratives in the Gospels of Matthew and Luke*. New York: Doubleday, 1993.

Brown, Raymond E. *The Death of the Messiah: From Gethsemane to the Grave: A Commentary on the Passion Narratives in the Four Gospels*. New York: Doubleday, 1994.

Davies, Eryl W. *Biblical Criticism: A Guide for the Perplexed*. London: Bloomsbury, 2013.

Dewey, Arthur J., and Robert J. Miller. *The Complete Gospel Parallels*. Salem, OR: Polebridge, 2012.

Friedman, Richard Elliott. *The Bible with Sources Revealed: A New View into the Five Books of Moses*. San Francisco: HarperSanFrancisco, 2003.

Hayes, John H., and Carl L. Holladay. *Biblical Exegesis: A Beginner's Handbook*. 3rd ed. Louisville, KY: Westminster John Knox, 2007.

McKenzie, Steven L., ed. *The Oxford Encyclopedia of Biblical Interpretation.* 2 vols. New York: Oxford University Press, 2013.

McKenzie, Steven L., and Stephen R. Haynes, eds. *To Each Its Own Meaning: An Introduction to Biblical Criticisms and Their Application.* Rev. and expanded ed. Louisville, KY: Westminster John Knox, 1999.

McKenzie, Steven L., and John Kaltner, eds. *New Meanings for Ancient Texts: Recent Approaches to Biblical Criticism and Their Applications.* Louisville, KY: Westminster John Knox, 2013.

7 The Uses of the Bible

Beal, Timothy, ed. *The Oxford Encyclopedia of the Bible and the Arts.* 2 vols. New York: Oxford University Press, 2015.

Beavis, Mary Ann, and Michael J. Gilmour, eds. *Dictionary of the Bible and Western Culture.* Sheffield: Sheffield Phoenix, 2012.

Bottigheimer, Ruth B. *The Bible for Children: From the Age of Gutenberg to the Present.* New Haven & London: Yale University Press, 1996.

Coogan, Michael. *God's Favorites: Judaism, Christianity, and the Myth of Divine Chosenness.* Boston: Beacon, 2019.

Dalton, Russell W. *Children's Bibles in America: A Reception History of the Story of Noah's Ark in US Children's Bibles.* New York: Bloomsbury T & T Clark, 2016.

The Encyclopedia of the Bible and Its Reception. Berlin: De Gruyter, 2009–.

Metzger, Bruce M., and Michael D. Coogan. *The Oxford Companion to the Bible.* New York: Oxford University Press, 1993.

Strawn, Brent A. *The Oxford Encyclopedia of the Bible and Law.* 2 vols. New York: Oxford University Press, 2015.

8 Biblical Concepts

Baden, Joel S. *The Book of Exodus: A Biography.* Princeton, NJ: Princeton University Press, 2019.

Coogan, Michael. "The Exodus from Egypt: A Deep Probe," pages 43–53 in *The Old Testament: A Very Short Introduction* (New York: Oxford University Press, 2008).

Friedman, Richard Elliott. *The Exodus: How It Happened and Why It Matters.* New York: HarperOne, 2017.

9 Biblical Values

Brawley, Robert L., ed. *The Oxford Encyclopedia of the Bible and Ethics.* 2 vols. New York: Oxford University Press, 2014.

Coogan, Michael. *God and Sex: What the Bible Really Says.* New York: Twelve, 2010.

Coogan, Michael. *The Ten Commandments: A Short History of an Ancient Text*. New Haven: Yale University Press, 2014.

de Villiers, Pieter G. R. "Violence," pages 384–390 in *The Oxford Encyclopedia of the Bible and Ethics*, Vol. 2 (ed. R. G. Brawley; New York: Oxford University Press, 2014).

Fagenblat, Michael. "The Concept of Neighbor in Jewish and Christian Ethics," pages 645–650 in *The Jewish Annotated New Testament* (ed. A.-J. Levine and M. Z. Brettler; New York: Oxford University Press, 2nd ed., 2017).

Meyers, Carol, ed. *Women in Scripture: A Dictionary of Named and Unnamed Women in the Hebrew Bible, the Apocryphal/Deuterocanonical Books, and the New Testament*. Boston: Houghton Mifflin, 2000.

Newsom, Carol A., Sharon H. Ringe, and Jacqueline E. Lapsley, eds. *Women's Bible Commentary*. 3rd ed. Louisville, KY: Westminster John Knox, 2012.

O'Brien, Julia M., ed. *The Oxford Encyclopedia of the Bible and Gender Studies*. 2 vols. New York: Oxford University Press, 2014.

ONLINE RESOURCES

Bible Odyssey. A multimedia open-access website by the Society of
Biblical Literature that focuses on important passages, people,
places, and events in the Bible. www.bibleodyssey.com

Oremus Bible Browser. An open-access concordance to several different
English translations. bible.oremus.org

Oxford Biblical Studies Online. A reference website with translations,
commentaries, encyclopedias, maps, illustrations, and many other
tools. www.oxfordbiblicalstudies.com

Project Torah and Biblical Scholarship. A historical and contextual
approach. Open access. theTorah.com

INDEX

For the benefit of digital users, indexed terms that span two pages (e.g., 52–53) may, on occasion, appear on only one of those pages.

Tables, figures and boxes are indicated by *t*, *f* and *b* following the page number